T0132276

#LoveYourself

A Guide to Awakening the Soul
and Putting the Ego to Sleep

Karen A. Baquiran

Tena M. Dodds

BALBOA.PRESS
A DIVISION OF HAY HOUSE

Balboa Press books may be ordered through booksellers or by contacting:

Balboa Press
A Division of Hay House
1663 Liberty Drive
Bloomington, IN 47403
www.balboapress.com
1 (877) 407-4847

Because of the dynamic nature of the Internet, any web addresses or links contained in this book may have changed since publication and may no longer be valid. The views expressed in this work are solely those of the author and do not necessarily reflect the views of the publisher, and the publisher hereby disclaims any responsibility for them.

The author of this book does not dispense medical advice or prescribe the use of any technique as a form of treatment for physical, emotional, or medical problems without the advice of a physician, either directly or indirectly. The intent of the author is only to offer information of a general nature to help you in your quest for emotional and spiritual well-being. In the event you use any of the information in this book for yourself, which is your constitutional right, the author and the publisher assume no responsibility for your actions.

Any people depicted in stock imagery provided by Getty Images are models, and such images are being used for illustrative purposes only.
Certain stock imagery © Getty Images.

Print information available on the last page.

ISBN: 978-1-9822-4380-7 (sc)
ISBN: 978-1-9822-4382-1 (hc)
ISBN: 978-1-9822-4381-4 (e)

Library of Congress Control Number: 2020903691

Balboa Press rev. date: 02/24/2020

This book is dedicated to my Bugs.
No matter where I am, your smiles and
laughter will always bring me home.

Table of Contents

Acknowledgements

To Zen (Agnes), Adam, Azul and the Sirian Light Council, Galactic Family from Sirius, Earth guides, HS, my cool Ego, Inner Child, Source, Angels and Archangels, for giving me the gift to express the wisdom you have blessed me with. This book wouldn't have been possible had you not been there to push me in shifting the world's perception as we know it.

To the people who have liked, shared and followed my page *Love Yourself – Movement,* thank you for your continuous support in my journey to self-love. It has been an honor to share messages of love to each of you.

Sophie Lefebvre (mon ange), la première fois que nous nous sommes rencontrées, j'ai tout de suite su que nous nous étions connues dans une autre vie. Vous m'avez guidée sur le chemin de ma croissance personnelle. Vous avez été un phare dans mon cheminement et je vous suis reconnaissante pour tout ce que vous m'avez apporté.

To marm and dad, thank you for always allowing me to be free to live my life. I cannot thank you enough for sacrificing your time of retirement to help take care of my bugs. You have been THE example of hard work and dedication while maintaining an active social life and keeping our family together. I am so appreciative for everything you have done for us and for supporting me unconditionally. Love you infinitely.

To my seestors and brothers, Carly, Pickle, Mario, Andy, I am so thankful for your love and support. You have seen me through the ugly and the beautiful and I appreciate everything you have done for me in my life. I love you all so much.

To Tony, What has been one of the most difficult decisions has turned into its own space of peace and friendship. I have always wanted us to be exactly where we are today. Though it took a lot of pain and suffering to get here, it was worth it. I am so lucky to have you in my life as my friend and co-parent. Love ya.

To Anto and Bruno, I have been fortunate to have you both as my second set of parents. You have always been so encouraging and supportive in everything I have ever done. To Anto, I am so grateful for our friendship and how we are there for one another. You're always the one person I can count on and I appreciate you for the sacrifices you have made for all of us. Love you both.

To the Baquiran, de las Alas, Mendoza, Ducusin, Colobong, and Austria family near and far, for your constant support and for always allowing me to be exactly who I am. I love you all so much.

To everyone who has left an imprint in my heart, my step-dogs: Bud and Coco, Beenders (Cherry, Ate Alma, Winnie, Ate Tess), Veronika Rao, JD Dodds, Autumn and Jamie, Dustin and Jill, Aunt Bonnie and Uncle Joey, Corey Caffo, Milynne Borason, Flores Family, Rita Wong, Richard Sandoval, Aina Arciaga, George Kong, Marvyn Capco, LJaye Pang, Braga, Theresa Fouyolle, Sarah Ann Brousseau, Ann Pascual, Divinia Agra, Luisa Sousa, Archie Kourakis, Cynthia Alleyne, Gullaci family, Frank and Sylvie, Mary Mancini, Jayesha Mistry, Christina Marcoux, Caroline Scanlon, Noy, Farhat Mirza, Anik Assanah, Laura Ann Elizabeth, Dana Grozdanova, Rheza Cayanong, Maria and Bill Russ, Christine Dahl, thank you for your love and support. We appreciate you being there and touching our life with your presence.

À ma famille de travail du CICL, je n'ai jamais rencontré des collègues aussi merveilleux. Vous rendez mon expérience de travail en radio-oncologie inoubliable. Vous m'avez tous apporté un grand soutien et je vous remercie de votre patience envers moi lors de la réalisation de ce projet.

To my divine soul counterpart, T-pac, I can't believe we finally frickin did it! When you came into my life, you had given me a priceless gift that had helped propel my life forward. That gift was love and hope and it was a driving force and motivation for me to live my best life. You've always seen me as the best version of myself and have waited patiently for me to align with her. You've dared me to do everything in the name of courage, especially in the times I was faced with the illusion of fear. I can't thank you enough for loving me through every trigger, ugly cry, and awkward moment. You have never judged me but have perfectly mirrored and held space for me to expand in extraordinary ways. Thank you for calling me to join you in this wild ride, where we get to do everything we've always dreamed of (including awkward youtube videos lol). I'm so grateful and fortunate to share my life with you as my partner, my equal and #rideordie. Thank you for loving the ET that I am. I love you, since forever. #OSG

Lastly, to my beautiful Bugs, Matthew and Julia, thank you for sharing your mommy with the rest of the world. It has been a privilege to have you as my greatest teachers. You are the only beings on this planet who know what my heart sounds like from the inside. I never thought I could do what I am doing, but after having you both, I know anything is possible. I promise that you will never live in the shadows of my life but only in my light. You make me believe in miracles every day and I love you both to the many infinite moons in the Universe and back.

Foreword

There are several examples of the divine principles of life and struggle that can be found in nature. Take metamorphosis, which in simplistic terms is a process wherein a caterpillar proceeds to transform into a butterfly. When closely examined, metamorphosis is a complicated process that involves more than just the shedding of layers, but includes the total death of an entity to be rebirthed into something new.

Major life transitions are metaphorically similar to metamorphosis.

Karen A. Baquiran's work *#LoveYourself - A Guide to Awakening the Soul and Putting the Ego to Sleep,* represents real life examples of a transformational process similar to that of metamorphosis. These series of short works represent the beginning stages of rebirth, involving a daily and growing separation from the old to a new life. Like the caterpillar transformation to pupa, as people we may reach plateaus in our lives or suddenly decide that what we are no longer serves us, which results in our need to change. Without giving reason, this need to transform may be seen as a choice or, like metamorphosis, something inevitable. Because these are the first stages of transition, there is other work to do like letting go and adapting to a new skin, before the entire transformational process is complete.

In my own career as a healthcare professional, I have worked with people and their families to adjust to new life circumstances and have assisted in the process to accept the often unsettling need to change. By no means is changing an easy feat, regardless of whether a life or death notice is attached. And so I commend those who willingly decide to make changes in their lives for the better, whether the reason is to be healthier, safer, or saner. Why continue to crawl when you have it in you to fly?

Carla Baquiran

Introduction – #LoveYourself – The Awakening

"At some point in our lives, we all long for home, to find our true selves, to be loved. What we don't always realize is that the power resides only within us. We are taught and conditioned by society to constantly seek healing outside of our own heart and soul. The power to heal our own wounds, to find our worth, to fully and unapologetically love ourselves out of the ceaseless fire of life, is ours and always has been. Sometimes it takes an enormous amount of suffering to come to this conclusion but once it's made, the world opens wide, we align with the Universe and from then on, anything and everything is possible. We find home, we find our true selves." –Tena M. Dodds

I wish I counted the times that I've picked at my brain and the amount of times I said I've had enough of this life. Had I paid more attention, maybe then I would have healed myself sooner. Not asking the right questions got me further from my awareness and I mistook ignoring my worth for normal. I've been awake during the storm and I stood there in the middle of a hurricane of confusing emotions that made me question my existence. I watched it all explode before me and I watched it happen not knowing how to fix it or how to resuscitate myself.

For the longest time I was a DNR (Do Not Resuscitate) case, but what I didn't know at the time was that there was still a fire burning in me that wanted to be ignited again. I fell in love with the idea that even though I had crumbled to the ground, I was given the opportunity to rebuild myself and it didn't matter who knew me before. But I was so far gone into this whirlwind of my emotional crisis that I suddenly didn't care what people thought anymore. I was always my harshest critic but the beauty of this entire journey held me in a place I never thought was possible.

I was always evolving into me, evolving from the seed that was planted long before I was ever fooled into believing that my life wasn't in my own hands. I've watched myself bleed and I've heard my inner cries through the pains in my body. I heard them cry through the aches of my thoughts that were continuously screeching forth into oblivion. I heard myself wonder in the dead of night, trying desperately to speak through my heartache, through the ball that was lodged permanently in my throat to keep me from screaming. I heard it so many times but I ignored it. I was taught to ignore it. I ignored it for so long that the last decade of my life consisted of merely existing, not living and sadly evolving into nothing. The numbness of my existence had overtaken me and I realized I had walked so far away from the soul that was stored deep in my core.

The sounds of everyday proclaimed, my attention was present, but the rhythm was never at par with the true beat of my heart. All at once I was avoiding pieces of the puzzle and every time I did, something else arose. I was so good at ignoring myself that I forgot who I was and I became a person I no longer recognized. I was there, in physical form, but mentally and emotionally checked out. I was faking my life, wanting to sleep the many hours of my sullen reality away. When I was awake, I didn't know what was real or what it meant to be happy anymore. I lived off the happiness and reality of others, and even though I never really connected with it, I went along with it anyway. It became my profession.

I thought that being loved for whatever given value of love was as good as it got, when in fact there was so much more to it. Pain ran deep through my veins and I watched my eyes age. I grew so far from knowing my worth. I was a stranger walking through life thinking this was it. I'm going to fake it for the rest of my life and I'll die not even knowing who I am or what my true potential is. I was so far gone that I couldn't even try to find me. I was buried under all the scar tissue, behind the walls that stored my emotional battles, trapped deep in a place of self-limbo.

I fell one moment and it was so hard. It was so hard that I jolted. What was it that the Universe wanted to show me? There was just something in the midst of my wondering that shook me back to life. I was shaken to my core so intensely that the walls surrounding my true self started crumbling one at a time. As each wall fell, I realized that I could resuscitate myself back into my very being because I was suddenly feeling emotions that I thought were dead within me. I was in control the whole time. It was I that walked away from my being.

I was digging through the rubble, knowing I was still in there somewhere, hiding, waiting to be found again. It was as though my heart started to beat but not to the tune I was used to. It started beating to something more familiar, something more innate. I felt it pounding stronger, pumping life through my veins, bringing myself back to life, and leading me to learn to be comfortable in my own skin that I longed to call home. I kept shaking through my newfound awareness and as one wall was torn down, I was soon filling in the holes that remained in their place. The holes seemed bottomless, but somewhere deep within me, I saw the light seeping through, bright enough to reconnect me with my lost soul. I had proof that there was hope and knew there was life left inside me. I started to bleed again but I knew I had to. It was the only way life would be brought back to my being. I knew that eventually it would stop again but only because I would be present enough to heal myself with the light that filled me eternally.

I wonder what happens to the people who are never found. How they continue to live in darkness, watching their false selves walk through life, unheard, sad, lost, and veiled. I broke through that barrier and I honored the girl that never lost hope. I was always in there, hoping for a cure, hoping to be found so I could come out and play. I wanted to smile but only because I finally found a reason to. I was tired of feeding that darkness within me and knew it was my time to find the light instead. I wanted to feel my true emotions because they belonged only to me. I crumbled and while digging through the rubble of my past, I found pieces of my true self waiting to be cradled, nurtured, and brought back to life.

I sprinkled lots of love into the remainder of the holes that still existed within me. I shed light on my pain and I allowed myself to feel it with the intent of going through the motions that I never thought were natural. A new journey begins in finding home within my soul. I started dealing with my pain but only at the pace I was comfortable with. This is all new to me. Every day, I honor myself for wanting this path, as not many people find themselves because they don't know where to look or where to begin.

My life is still a work in progress but I love that I can do anything I want because it's mine to fix, it's mine to love and it's mine to live. The color is slowly coming back into my face and in my body. I've decided to let go and allow the darkness to seep away like a mist that had chronically kept me blinded in sadness. I stood there, no longer chained to my agony, and with my own personal power my heart began to beat to its endless rhythm, filling my soul with the color of light, the color of love, the color of my life.

Chapter 1
Letting Go

"She walked without apology
Exhaled deeply and surrendered
She let go
This was the beginning of her unbecoming."

Karen A. Baquiran

Introduction: Letting Go

"When faced with a life situation or problem that makes us uncomfortable, we have a few choices. We can resist what is happening, causing internal pain, turmoil, and frustration. We can change it. And if change isn't possible, we can accept it as if we have chosen it, surrender to what is and live through it the best way we know how, building strength along the way until we gain the capacity for change." –Tena M. Dodds

I felt dead inside. It was a realization I addressed when I lay in my bed in the middle of night. The very things that I thought would fulfill my life were the exact same things that were killing my joy. And that was my fault because I let it come this far. I made those very decisions thinking it would bring me joy, when it actually did the opposite. I kept making excuse after excuse that everything was fine and I was the problem because I couldn't appreciate what I had. While that was partially true, I was responsible for the problems I was having and something had to change.

This realization made me sulk because I didn't want to deal with it or face it or say it out loud. I was scared to acknowledge what was happening and face myself and all my fears because that meant I had to address everything about my current life situation. I had no idea how to express myself. All I could feel was guilt; that I had the potential to hurt so many people that I loved. Shame that I felt this deep need to reveal the truth I denied for so long. It came to a point where the turmoil of my unhappiness stirred so hard inside that I got swallowed up by the vortex until it exploded in my face.

I avoided change because I didn't know how to do it. I was taught to accept things for what they are and in my perception, it felt like my feelings didn't matter. It was always about how it looked to the public and that if I smiled, it would hide the chaos lying underneath. I lived with this unhealthy coping mechanism until my mind went mad and my face stopped cooperating at faking it. Pretending I was happy was just not an option anymore. My body wouldn't let me do it; it was in total resistance to my current life. I had to adapt to this change.

So what now? Do I repeat the same familial, ancestral, societal and generational pattern so that it never goes away and continues to self-perpetuate through my own children as well? Or should I fucking do something about it and be the one to break the chain, to stop it now from ever repeating again and teach my children how to stand in their truth, how to do what makes them happy and not what other people think they *should* do? The choice was easy: it had to end.

This journey has taught me that difficult situations are always arising. We're responsible for what we do and how we react to them, pushing through the storm to eventually find our way out and let it all go. I knew deep down that it wasn't right that I was always putting myself last. For the longest time, I didn't have enough self-worth to even believe that I deserved anything. My needs always came last, if they were ever addressed at all, and I was ok with that until now.

I didn't take drastic action right away in my decision to change, but it took just an ounce of awareness to make me start unveiling my truth and standing up for myself. I had extensive learning to do in letting go of old patterns and ways of thinking if I really wanted things to change. I never had the intention of drastically transforming my entire life; I thought the path I was on was supposed to make me happy. Isn't that what we're all told? If you do everything right and follow along, you'll be happy one day just like everybody else!

What a relief it was to finally learn that I had control over something, when I had gone through life thinking I had to accept that I was just an unhappy person who had little to no standards. It took a lot of time and a strong will to let go of everything that didn't serve me anymore. That included friendships and relationships, negative thought forms, unhealthy coping mechanisms, the old stories of what I believed was my identity and tons more.

It felt like I had to undo everything I've ever learned about life and what it means to truly be happy. That everything I was taught may have worked for others but it sure as hell didn't work for me anymore. I had to release it all, deprogram from the matrix, and examine my false belief systems and societal conditioning that led me here to this crossroad. It was a long road in unraveling endless layers but in the end, I finally found the space to breathe, the space to be freely, unapologetically me.

I've reminisced to old times and not once did I think I could ever get here to this place of truly being happy deep down in my heart and soul. It took tons of hard work and personal reflection but once I got in the process of getting to know myself, everything on the superficial surface naturally faded on its own and the real me was finally exposed. Feeling dead inside was a distant memory. I was now excitedly anticipating a fresh start and a new life, a do-over if you will, in which I am the master creator of my own story and I get to choose how it ends.

1.1 Letting Go

"If there's one thing I've learned about life, it's that it goes on. We either roll with it or get left behind." –Tena M. Dodds

Whether we've been deceived or praised or hurt or happy or hated or loved, the ongoing forward motion of life continues to move with or without us. As humans with runaway monkey brains, we tend to focus on instances that keep us stuck in a particular moment. We tend to remain mentally or emotionally trapped in an old memory that clearly keeps us from moving forward.

Unfortunately, some of us can remain in that particular moment even if it happened decades ago. But how do we move on? How do we get the courage to say *I will not remain in a prison of mental slavery and pain?* To put it blandly, we move on and forward because we make that decision and commitment to do so. Because the mind can be so complex, it is our willingness to heal that drives us. If it's guilt that is holding us back, then that guilt is seeping through into our mind, heart, and soul straight into our everyday lives. We end up bathing in this toxicity and it ends up dictating how we think, feel, and express ourselves. We become so deeply imprisoned by an old situation, stagnant in bitterness and keeping our focus on what went wrong and the importance of being right.

By bringing our attention to what is happening right now, we become present, and if for a second we can forget what happened in the past, we become able to feel and breathe love into this present moment, to celebrate life as it stands, and appreciate the preciousness of every day. Working on letting things go can help establish a healthier mind set, a healthier body, and a healthier heart. Because our mind is no longer holding onto a thing of the past, our focus is on today's life and we can live it to the fullest. Life moves on, but it is you who decides whether to join it or not.

1.2 Letting Go

"Every person we encounter comes into our lives to teach us. Whether our relationship ends on a good or bad note is irrelevant if we're open to the lesson. Sometimes we don't get the closure we're looking for, but in the end, we are stronger and wiser for having approached the situation with an open mind." –Tena M. Dodds

Fights happen when opposing ideals come to the forefront and we're left to confront and stand up for our beliefs. When everything blows up and out of proportion, communication can turn to arguing and yelling, to the point where both parties have stopped listening. The egos of both parties get bruised so deeply that it may end in a hurtful exchange and when it all unfolds, nothing positive comes from the fight and we're left without closure. When this happens, we feel that it's almost impossible to move on because we put so much focus on how the other person reacted and what they unjustly said. We go in a state of protecting ourselves by justifying that we didn't do anything wrong. They were wrong! As time passes, sometimes there is no resolution or a genuine apology. So what do we do when getting closure is impossible?

It isn't worth it to suffer from a situation when either party has no intention to communicate and listen to the other. What ends up happening thereafter is that we may find ourselves chronically making up scenarios in our head about what everything means, analyzing the situation over and over, and coming up with our own conclusion because we have lost control over it. We desperately seek answers even if we make them up, so we can fill up the blank spaces with the little control we have. However, doing this can really take a toll on our body and mental health, even to the point of becoming obsessed.

I always ask myself, "If they can't give me the time of day, why do I let the pain eat me alive? Why am I dwelling on this past issue when I could be living happily right now? Why do I allow myself to feel like this circumstance is taking over my life? Why am I wasting my time thinking about issues that hurt me and being so consumed with the comebacks I never said?"

We all find ourselves in these scenarios from time to time where we replay what happened repeatedly in our mind. We drive ourselves crazy wondering what we could have done differently to prevent it or even to solidify what we were expressing, but we need to recognize that every event and how it unfolds is supposed to happen. It is the Universe's way of:

1. helping us to learn from what happened.
2. making us stronger from these relationships.
3. making us challenge ourselves to process issues differently and to let it go if it doesn't serve us.
4. teaching us to respond consciously instead of reacting.

There is a lesson to be learned in everything we go through in life, especially from the challenges with other human beings. So, the next time we find ourselves in a similar situation, we will know better than to fall into the same toxic cycle. We will be able to handle the outcome in a healthier manner, instead of feeling sorry for ourselves and assuming a false story we convinced ourselves of. There comes a point when we have to let it go and learn not to hold a grudge.

The people that show up in our lives that make us crazy are there to teach us these lessons and we are there to teach them the same. These people are here to teach us something, to act as a mirror to show us who we are and what we need to heal. So whatever the relationship was, we can appreciate the experience and the wisdom we've gained once we step outside of what happened. When we finally move out of it and reflect, we'll see how much better we are now that we have the capacity to observe what happened and not feel the need to control the unsaid words. We will see that they've served a purpose in our lives and that our lives are much richer because of what they have taught us. In the end, these lessons help us to find our happiness in the present moment and bring a sense of awareness about the way we think and how corroded our thoughts have become when we're running play-by-plays. Instead, we should bombard ourselves with love, patience, and wisdom and create a healthy space for an open, unclouded mind. Let it go.

1.3 Letting Go

"We're conditioned as children, especially as girls, to put others needs before our own, to give out more than we receive. But this creates an unequal balance and we end up depleted in the end. It's absolutely a must to take care of yourself before you give your time or energy to anyone else; you cannot give what you don't have." –Tena M. Dodds

Some of us tend to be natural caregivers and may find it's our duty to care for others before ourselves, but it's time to take a break for a moment and reflect on our own needs. It may seem natural to make sure that everyone else is comfortable, but who is looking out for us? We all need to refresh and re-evaluate every so often otherwise we'll end up depleted and broken.

When people are lucky enough to be generously taken care of by someone, sometimes instead of expressing gratitude, they feel entitled and they end up taking for granted or even abusing the person who cares for them. How do we rectify a situation like that? People will treat us the way we allow them to, so if we're taking someone's crap all the time, it's probably because we let them crap on us! It is the curse of the enabler, but it is never too late to take our power back.

Changing the way people treat us can be challenging, especially if it's been happening for a long time. However, fixing the problem would do a whole lot of good for our sanity, well-being, and our relationships in general. Sometimes people don't even realize that they're being mean or ungrateful, so it's necessary to tell them that our feelings are hurt by the way they treat us.

We all deserve to be treated with courtesy and respect. It's so important to look out for ourselves because we can't trust that someone will do it for us and we cannot take care of others if we aren't 100%.

It's healthy to make ourselves a priority sometimes and I would go as far as to say, all the time. It's also ok to say no. No is a complete sentence. If you want to test the healthiness of your relationship, practice saying no and pay attention to the response you get. If you're like me and you suffer from disease to please syndrome, this is no easy task. But think about it, other people have no problem saying "no" to us, so what's stopping us? Guilt, worry that we'll let them down or hurt their feelings or not live up to their expectations… but who's feeling bad for us when we're draining ourselves by giving everything? It's time that we, as caregivers, take on that role for ourselves.

Holding onto these emotions is a waste of our precious energy and we are the only one suffering. If people make us feel bad, we must be vocal and tell them to stop. And if they get mad at us for finally voicing our thoughts, that isn't our problem and we need to re-evaluate the relationship. We should never be someone's doormat.

Breaking old habits can take time so be patient with yourself. Practicing mindfulness helps us become aware of how we're being treated, and creating boundaries for ourselves is essential in any relationship to protect our energy, time, and space.

Every single one of us deserves all the care, happiness, and love in this world. I know it can be hard because of the feelings of guilt, but we must train our minds to not allow the guilt to take over and manipulate us into doing things we don't want to do. Don't let someone's desperate antics control your life. By making this simple change, by saying no, we can alter their next move and before you know it, you'll be free from guilt and people pleasing behaviors. We should make ourselves a priority once in a while. It's not selfish, it's necessary.

1.4 Letting Go

"When confronted with fear and hate, let me lead with compassionate love and forgiveness. Let me see clearly our innate Divine oneness rather than our false sense of separateness. Let my heart be wide open and my gentle spirit be the example of what it means to value all of life." –Tena M. Dodds

My wish is for my children to develop a strong sense of courage, compassion, gentleness, and wisdom so that they have a solid foundation and take on the cruel world with the power of love, hope, peace, joy, and kindness. We're living in a society where we're bombarded by the media and their perception of what makes us beautiful and happy. People are becoming brainwashed and conditioned into social norms that are causing our society to deteriorate from lack of self-worth. It's up to us to teach our children that happiness and beauty starts within the self and not the constant external-seeking behavior portrayed by the media and society.

I'm making it a point in my parenting to make sure that my kids are both able to recognize their value and that it doesn't matter what society tells them. All that matters is that they're happy with who they are. Building a solid foundation for self-worth is so important because everyone tends to get lost in the pressure of looking a certain way or having certain things.

My children are half Filipino and half Italian. It's inevitable for them to know that they're considered minority because of a simple facial observation. They look a little different but what they need to recognize is that it's not a bad thing to have physical and cultural differences. It makes them unique and beautiful.

I grew up as a Filipino in Quebec, the French province of Canada, and lived in a Francophone majority neighborhood. With the physical differences (as well as being one of the only English-speaking families in the neighborhood), my family and I endured ridicule. We were exposed to racism because of our slanted eyes and we were considered stupid because we couldn't speak their language.

For the longest time, I didn't want to learn to speak French, probably from the trauma of the verbal and sometimes physical abuse from the neighbors. I basically didn't want to learn the language of the enemy. Somewhere down the line I realized that I wasn't any better than them because what they had done to me, allowed me to do the same to them. I allowed their unkind acts to control the way I viewed all French people and how I lived my life. That was never fair to me. I stopped living because of fear and because I was unable to recognize my own self-worth.

Twenty-nine years later, I courageously decided to forgive the so-called enemy and learn the French language. I stopped being afraid because I grew enough confidence to let go of my fear. I had to forgive the racists because I understood that it was their insecurities and ignorance that caused them to attack us. I was able to use my compassion in understanding that they just didn't know any better. The only factor that determined the difference between me and them was that I knew better.

I wanted to challenge myself a little more, so I applied to a French hospital and after hours of practicing a language I barely understood, I got hired, and it validated the idea that I could do anything. If I wasn't going to challenge myself, the hate that I'd developed for the people who treated me badly wouldn't make me any better than they were. I soon realized that the fear I had coming into work would ease because I worked with the most incredible team (mostly French speaking people) who welcomed me with open arms despite my own physical and language differences.

I was challenged at a young age for being what was seen as inferior because of my looks and because of my mother tongue. I embrace the child that had to endure this and learn the hard way. My spirit is stronger because of this. I know my worth now and knowing what it feels like to get the short end of the stick because of who I am just empowers me more to be the better person.

I can forgive them because I realized that their insecurity and ignorance was never my problem or my reality. I am compassionate and understanding and I will be a positive force and example for my children. I hope that they never have to go through that, but it's a possibility because they have physical attributes that come from me. I can only teach them to be proud of who they are and where they come from so that if one day their peers were to attack with negative words, I could only hope that they respond, "I am a child born in love and I know my value. It doesn't matter what you say about me because I know that I'm beautiful and that I'm enough."

1.5 Letting Go

"I don't always believe in forgive and forget but I do believe in forgive, learn, and let go." –Tena M. Dodds

I never understood the concept of forgiveness, especially when an apology never came before it. I always thought you could only forgive if the person said they were sorry. If the sorry never came, a grudge would be held, and even if they did apologize, I felt like I couldn't forget what happened. I had a difficult time letting it go especially when I felt like I was treated unjustly. I couldn't find it in my heart to forgive and I easily played it off like I didn't care but would talk about what happened so much and pretended like I let it go when I obviously didn't.

I used to be that person who would hold a grudge I had towards someone and think "Ugh! Who cares about that fucking loser!" But I obviously did care if I still had the sour attitude. I'd hold onto it, pretending like I was tough but underneath it all I was giving my power to someone who I assumed didn't care about me. I was the only one who was angry, so I was the only one suffering. We have the tendency to marinate in our own problems because we proudly refuse to forgive, which results in a lack of moving forward. We carry that emotional baggage with us and if there are several grudges being held within us, it takes a toll on how we carry ourselves in the world and leaves very little room to grow.

Forgiveness is the key to moving on and releasing the negative energy we have felt in our own victimhood. Sometimes we hold back forgiveness out of spite, as if forgiving someone is offering them a gift that they don't deserve, when in truth it's not a gift to them at all, but instead a gift to ourselves. It's the gift of releasing the heavy burden of bitterness and anger and releasing the past in order to make space for living fully in the present with our whole heart.

Even if we find ourselves stuck in an unfortunate circumstance, we can hold onto the knowing that as time passes, the pain will lessen. But in the meantime, we should feel our emotions all the way through, validate them, and allow them to process fully. When we feel that we are ready to release the negative feelings, the ultimate test of strength is really in forgiveness, especially in the case where we never receive an apology.

We should stay true to the fact that we don't have to forget what happened to us, we don't have to accept that person back into our lives, we don't even have to let them know they are forgiven. But we can look at it as another life lesson to be learned. There is no point in reacting to the negativity because then we're only contributing to the karmic ripple effect, causing drama when the ripple effect should stop at us. Instead, we can respond, thoughtfully with intent and mindfulness. There is a difference between having a reactionary response and responding mindfully.

I can think back to a lot of the things that I've been angry about over the years but after I forgave them, I look at it and think that it really wasn't so bad. The things we once thought were horrendous become interestingly laughable because we are mentally, emotionally, and spiritually in a better place. When we can reflect on a problem and have no emotional response towards it, that's when we know the lesson has been learned and we have healed.

I don't believe in forgive and forget, but I believe in forgive, learn, and let go. Forgiveness is the key to a huge door to freedom. These problems are a way to have us look deep within ourselves. What is it that needs to be healed? What is it that needs to be learned? What is it that needs to happen so that I can be free from this grudge that I am responsible for holding? I may be the devil to someone, but what they don't know is that I also may be their biggest lesson.

1.6 Letting Go

"Letting go is an art form in which we learn to release the pain, anger, resentment, and bitterness that so often burdens our hearts from past experiences. The more we release, the more space is created for love and joy and freedom to enter." –Tena M. Dodds

Yesterday was the first Thanksgiving where I completely understood its true meaning. Our family had a get-together and in the spirit of this holiday, I felt a powerful feeling of gratitude for my family on a much deeper level. Going through this spiritual journey and seeing life on a greater scale, I saw this holiday as a beautiful opportunity to reconnect and it was as wonderful as I had thought it would be.

I reconnected with family I had lost touch with for a few years. We went through this terrible ordeal when I got married and we sadly went our separate ways. I was continuously mourning the time we lost because for as close as we once were, our bond, sadly, had changed. And for both parties, it felt like there was an unbearable strain that was impossible to forget.

On this journey, I have learned to just be as I am and not to let my ego get the best of me. So, with a lot of love and a full heart, I consciously let go of the drama and forgave what had happened and took accountability for what I contributed to the matter. I acknowledged my pain and I acknowledged my anger and as I surrendered, I said to these feelings, "You no longer serve a purpose in what happened. I can happily say that I am okay now and I thank you for being part of me. I can put you away because I am ready to move on." I could not have a relationship with my estranged family if I couldn't give 100% of myself to them.

Letting it go and learning from it really allowed me to open up to them more than I thought it would. I was terrified that it was going to be awkward, but I didn't let myself be that, instead, I was able to shift so that they felt it was safe to follow. It felt natural and I felt a positive shift in our new forming bond. Allowing my love and light to shine through broke the strain and I am so thankful that we allowed one another back into each other's lives. The void I had in my heart filled quickly and I was immediately liberated.

Through this journey, I have learned that we can sometimes lose the people we are close to. It doesn't matter how we fell out of touch, but we need to acknowledge that it happened because although sad, it is a part of our story. With a lot of faith and love, we can reconnect when both parties are ready and willing. Instead of dwelling on the time we lost, I am filled with gratitude for the time that'll be gained.

I believe in the power of change and self-reflection for the benefit of ourselves and those around us. I believe that being able to truly forgive and let go can heal all things. I am thankful for my experiences and in the spirit of this holiday, thankful that I never lost faith and thankful that they didn't lose faith in me.

1.7 Letting Go

"Becoming free of mental slavery is a decision followed by a series of everyday choices to be honest with ourselves. Being honest requires looking closely at our thoughts and behaviors at every turn and monitoring why we do the things we do, always with the intention of doing better next time." –Tena M. Dodds

How do we reach a positive state of mental health? It takes a lot of unbecoming to get there, letting go of everything we thought we were and everything we thought we knew. It requires a great deal of will-power and self-awareness, but unfortunately some of us have a hard time fighting through our demons because we get so caught in the web of stories we tell ourselves. How can we reach this level of mental stability and maintain it without ego getting in the way to sabotage? It takes a lot of patience and practice to become aware of our own thoughts and the way we perceive information.

Naturally anyone would feel like crap when presented with an unfortunate circumstance. However, with a healthy mind, we can feel our initial feelings and take a step back because we know on a deeper level that what we feel is temporary. We then make the conscious decision to not be consumed by outside circumstances. We remain solid in who we are, knowing that everything is temporary and everything that happens to us usually is happening for us, for our growth and evolution. In doing so, we also make the effort to move forward from it and not dwell on the issues. By allowing ourselves to remain steady, we can accept the situation for what it is and let ourselves learn from it as opposed to letting it break us into an emotional tailspin.

People with a healthy mind make mistakes but they take responsibility for their actions instead of blaming others. And because they take responsibility, they are also able to learn from their mistakes as it becomes a natural process in their healing. If change is part of the situation, they embrace whatever comes their way. They don't freak out for long periods or complain about it either. It is the acceptance that change is a necessary part of life, it is part of the journey that they're embarking on. When resistance persists, there is suffering. When surrender happens, so does the flow of life.

Mentally healthy people are completely aware of everything; therefore, they are aware of their ego and how the ego functions. It may take a lot to piss them off as they know they get to choose not to react, but instead, respond thoughtfully. They think before they act and live their lives guided by what serves their highest good. They act selflessly for others and are never looking to get anything in return but also have adequate boundaries in place to protect themselves. They are not bothered by being alone, sometimes they even prefer it, and they do not care what other people think of them because they're comfortable in their own skin. They practice non-judgment of others and themselves and are teachers for those in need of guidance.

Becoming mentally healthy is an act of choice. By making the time to retrain our brain, we can become more aware of what triggers our ego to react and we can prevent its dangerous potential to disrupt our inner peace. It should be made a practice to encourage the self to realize its wholeness and that we are enough as we are. And just knowing that can lead us into a new world altogether. In simply taking control of our lives, the possibilities of mental freedom are endless.

1.8 Letting Go

"I surrender to the moment, to the feelings that are arising and just hold on. Because I'm tired of fighting, tired of pushing so hard all the time. In fact, I'm utterly exhausted mentally, emotionally, and physically. I just want to sit and feel and let whatever happens, happen. I don't think there's any quick fix or solution. It just is. And I'm just going to be. Surrendering. Breathing. Feeling. Being." –Tena M. Dodds

I surrender.

I've been going through a phase recently where I feel completely uninspired and have the worst case of writer's block. It bothers me that I'm creatively barren and I don't know why. I'm trying to stay out of my head because the internal dialogue in my mind is building up so much pressure to perform because I have an audience waiting for me. I started doodling in my notebook and found myself writing these questions: Am I losing my creative touch? Does it matter if I don't publish anything today? Would people notice? Would people stop following my page because I'm creatively uninspired?

While writing these questions down, I actually started a live conversation with my ego. "Is it absolutely necessary to make me feel bad right now?" My ego came out to join the conversation in the form of insecurity. The internal conversation made me question myself and my ability to write.

I am not easily frustrated, but I must admit that it did frustrate me that I allowed myself to fall into the trap and illusion of pressure. It's crazy how our thoughts can get the best of us and if we're unable to catch the one thought that ripples into multiple other thoughts, we end up going in a downward spiral of negative thought-forms. It's a game of irrational vs. rational thoughts and thinking this illusion is real when it's certainly not. I can literally catch my internal dialogue and see how I'm being so hard on myself. Usually there are feelings of guilt attached to these negative thought-forms.

I've been able to catch my triggered response when thinking this way and it makes me get out of my bubble to observe what's happening. Catching these thoughts can easily eradicate any further internal damage. In my case, I was feeling inadequate because I felt like I wasn't living up to the expectations of the audience following my blog. I felt like it was my duty to serve others and I couldn't deliver. But why was I feeling that way? No one asked me to do this blog in the first place. So, I was able to assess that this imagined duty I made up was my ego.

I surrendered to my lack of inspiration. It made me reflect on the possible outcomes. If this was to be the last of my writing experience, would I be happy with what I have accomplished thus far? Yes, I am. Then that should be enough for me to feel adequate and not feed a false story line that I made up in my head. I have done enough, and inspiration will come when the pressure lifts and I surrender to the block. I am responsible to let it go, to be happy with my accomplishments and feel the pressure lift. I am enough.

I believe this bump in the road is just a gentle reminder to stay humble. It's a reminder to be grateful. It's a reminder to embrace my expression and freedom to do so, to enjoy the time I have with my children before I go back to work. It's a reminder to look out the window and allow the light of the sunlight to touch my face, to breathe in the sweet air. It's a reminder to let the light from my own soul shine forth to its infinite potential. This is the part of life we take for granted. We worry so much about our shortcomings when in fact we should appreciate the abundance of life that is right here in front of us. That is inspiring.

1.9 Letting Go

"Awakening to the truth of who we are is liberation. Beyond the ego lies infinite freedom and abundance. But so many people are only willing to touch the surface of life, afraid to let down the mask protecting their insecurities, staying trapped by fear and ego, ignoring their intuition, unknowingly causing themselves undue suffering and depriving themselves of salvation." –Tena M. Dodds

Once upon a time, I had an ego that I didn't know I could control. In fact, I don't think a lot of people know they can control it. Looking back, it was a lot of maintenance in keeping the ego battery alive. I was always so tough, and I wasn't afraid to let people know it. And in keeping up with the tough guy reputation, we must use up a lot of ego battery, a lot of energy to be there all the time, mask on, on guard and waiting for anything to piss us off. The truth is that there's a super sensitive guarded heart underneath the tough exterior and the mask of ego is only there to protect it. I think this is true for a lot of tough guys out there.

Now I sit here and giggle because I'm so far from the person who used to be on persistent guard. I acknowledged my ego because it is and always will be a part of me but decided that it has made enough appearances in the last three decades and now it was time to take a break. Sometimes it comes out for a peek but never for too long. The practice of recognizing my ego's voice becomes a normal part of my everyday routine and if things happen that would trigger the ego; I can automatically become the observer of my thoughts instead of losing myself within them.

There is nothing more liberating than the feeling of knowing that I don't have to be angry anymore for unhealthy amounts of time, that I don't have to lose my shit or get offended or act tough or hostile or be aggressive or judgmental or live in hate or be a downer reveling in my own pity party. I can sit back and enjoy my life and enjoy my higher-self. I can enjoy my freedom to love unconditionally, laugh from my soul, and look at everything from the eyes of soul, not from ego. When we look through the eyes of our soul, our views broaden and there are no limits to living. In the eyes of ego, all we see is what we want to see and usually that entails tunnel vision and not much else beyond the surface.

Ego is always on the prowl, waiting for opportunity to pounce. Always on edge, checking our backs for knives, gossipers, and haters. Always ready for attack. It's so stressful even thinking about it. When we're sitting with drama or problems upon problems because we get easily offended or angry, we should take a step back and think about ourselves and our reactions. We should forget who made us feel like this, but instead, look at how we allowed ourselves to feel this way. No one can make us feel something without our permission.

If we're always feeling attacked or under serious stress, our egos are simply reveling in our negative realities. The ego loves drama, it lives for it. Let's decide right now that we're going to stand up to this force and understand that we have the power to control it, lock it behind us, and finally open the door to freedom. We don't have to act tough anymore, we don't have to wear a fake mask… It's so exhausting anyway. Let our soul show us the new vision of clarity and true freedom.

1.10 Letting Go

"Your thoughts create your reality so whatever you're thinking, positively or negatively, consciously or unconsciously, is brought to life in your world, sometimes in ways you can't yet see. If you think you can't, then you won't. The battle is already lost before it even started." –Tena M. Dodds

In an ideal world, there would be no drama or suffering if people were aware of their thoughts and realized that they didn't need to believe every thought that passed by. They would understand the concept of taking responsibility and control of the force behind the quality of their thoughts. It would obviously be ideal to live in peace and harmony rather than in a toxic cycle of self-destruction and sabotage. If everyone were to take responsibility for their actions and pull their own weight for the greater good of society, what kind of a world would we live in?

We all know the toxic thinkers, the self-sabotager, the negative Nancy, the over-analyzer, the victim, the person who says they always have bad luck or a black cloud over their head, etc. I know this person because I used to be that person. We all need to be held responsible for the way we choose to think because our thoughts turn to actions and affect everyone around us. We can place blame all we want, but ultimately, it's the perception of our thoughts that make up the world we live in.

Understanding this concept can take time but once it's understood, it becomes a huge game changer. To comprehend the power we hold by taking control of our thoughts, is truly life altering. What we conceive in our thoughts will be brought to life if we apply it.

My girlfriend is an example of someone who has gone through hell and back. She has suffered from addiction, the loss of both parents and other loved ones, has debilitating chronic illnesses that have compromised her quality of life, an abusive marriage that has stripped her of everything imaginable. And still, despite her physical and emotional pain and suffering, she makes the commitment everyday to not get swallowed up in victimhood but instead chooses to make the best of her life and appreciate her experiences. It boggles my mind how she woke up and owned up to her life every single day.

It made me reflect on my life, where our experiences were nowhere similar and I became a prisoner of victimhood. Her strength and vigor for life inspired me to take responsibility for my life because if someone in her position were able to rise above what she had been through, then I'd be stupid not to follow. It's people like my girlfriend who inspire me everyday to wake up and make choices to commit to my own happiness and not focus on the reasons or negativity that have the potential to stop me from living.

We are the masters of our minds. We have control over every thought to believe it or change it. This is the key to the quality of our life. All we must do is take back control and choose to respond mindfully instead of reacting negatively. Some people blame everyone and anything for their poor misfortunes in life instead of taking responsibility but that is their choice. I will choose differently. Most of the time, it isn't worth the extended pain and suffering. Why should we tire ourselves for something so petty and sometimes out of our control, when we can choose to live as happy as we allow ourselves to? My girlfriend is the example of this and knowing what she's been through only motivates me to embody that inner power and make the drastic change to let go of circumstance and own my life.

1.11 Letting Go

"Caregivers must get out of the mindset that they have to put others before themselves at all times. This is a fallacy that is destroying well-meaning people in our culture. Do you notice that it's always the 'good ones' who get incurable or chronic illnesses and/or pass away before their time? This is not an accident; it's due to constantly neglecting the self and their own needs." –Tena M. Dodds

Alone time. I think everyone needs to take mental health days and quarantine themselves to reassess the 24/7 incessant chatter that goes on in our minds and take a break from the constant stimulation from the outside world. When we're out of an environment that engulfs our everyday lives, it can put everything into perspective. It isn't a selfish act to want to be alone. In fact, it's so important to take care of ourselves before we can take care of anyone else.

If we're a natural caregiver, we can't take care of others if we're not 100%. We should always be able to give ourselves some time even if it means hiding in a bathroom stall for a few minutes just to have some silence. We are entitled to escape the craziness of our everyday lives. Just to be able to drown out the noise makes a huge difference when recharging ourselves back to health.

Life passes us by so quickly and if we're always caught in the chaos, we may lose our minds to all the noise. But if we can physically take ourselves out of it just to have a different environment, we'll expose ourselves to healthier energy. If you are a master at silencing your mind amid chaos then, by all means, go for it! But by taking ourselves out, even just briefly, it allows us to reset and offset the buildup of stress. Taking care of ourselves, allows us to get back in there and see things from a healthier perspective.

I always encourage alone time. Sometimes as parents we feel guilty for abandoning ship but honestly, if we're getting lost in the everyday shuffle, then we need a change before it drives us crazy. Don't listen to the people who judge, as that's their problem, not yours. A healthy parent means healthy kids. Don't fall for the guilt trip because we're not weak; we're simply taking care of ourselves by creating the positive energy and space for everyone. Choosing to clear our minds or take time off is a huge step in a healthy direction.

There's no sense in going nutty when we can easily take a time-out. Adults need time-out too! Taking care of other people is great if the caregiver is healthy. It's amazing when we can get out of our minds for once and just be, it's not selfish. We are worth the sacrifice and silence if it means we are doing it to maintain the quality of our lives and therefore, the lives of our children and everyone around us.

1.12 Letting Go

"At times, you may feel devoid of your own strength and will to keep going. In those times, it's important to look to people that inspire you. Draw inspiration from their endurance, let it hold you up and propel you forward until you find your own again." –Tena M. Dodds

There are people in this world that go through immense amounts of pain, suffering, and sadness but somehow, they manage to keep going. These are the people that inspire me to stop feeling sorry for myself and are the driving force behind my own endurance. Endurance is what keeps us going when we feel we have nothing left. When it comes to life lessons, we either prolong the suffering or realize that we don't have to suffer through the pain; we can surrender to it and learn from it. If we choose to prolong it by feeling sorry for ourselves, it'll keep coming back to haunt us until we're ready to understand the true meaning.

Every now and then we find ourselves in a place where we feel like we aren't strong enough to get over something. And as we contemplate the reasons for its existence in our lives, we need to find the strength to endure it and deal with it head on. It sounds easy when you read it, but it takes a lot of effort to face yourself and your victimhood, to stop blaming your circumstances and take responsibility.

We sometimes justify our words or actions, or lack thereof, in a way that is convenient, but we need to stop making excuses. Life doesn't come with a manual, but one thing is for sure: when we are being pushed further into what seems like an endless and painful detour, there is always hope. But we must consciously look for and find the silver linings to help push us forward. In doing so, the real beauty of life will reveal itself, and we'll appreciate with gratitude the little things that we usually take for granted.

Continue to endure, to push through when all seems lost and use this endurance to better understand life. It may seem that everything is working against you but slowly you are gaining strength. Opening your eyes every morning, waking up and making the effort to push yourself beyond what you feel you can do, is a sign of your willingness and strength to keep going another day. Be proud of yourself.

We must find it in us to keep going despite how awful we may feel at times. Sometimes just finding a reason to smile and holding that smile for 17 seconds will help shift our attitude in a positive direction. Let's continue to walk with our heads held high so that we don't miss the beauty of what life shows us. There is always someone who is going through a tough time. Keep in mind that there are so many who have pushed hard enough past their pain and succeeded, triumphed, and survived. Let them be your inspiration to do better when you're struggling to find your strength. Endure. You never know who you will inspire.

1.13 Letting Go

"I wish I could show you the amazing beauty that stands before me. It is pure unadulterated Love at its core, radiating outward and entrancing all that come near with its majesty. With stardust dancing through its veins, with an essence of Divine Light filling every cell, with a soul full of magic and mystery, it is not broken. It is whole and has always been whole. Hold on, sweet friends. Hold on and you will see, one day, the beautiful light that is you." –Tena M. Dodds

In times when you've lost hope,
Your pain wants to be healed.
In times when you feel lost,
Your spirit longs to be found.
In times when you feel sadness,
Your happiness begs to be free.
In times when you're at war with life,
Your anger aches for peace.
In times when you feel deceived,
Your life seeks the truth.
In times when you feel it is the end,
Your higher self looks for a new beginning.
In times when hate is the answer,
Your soul longs to be loved.

I've battled anxiety and depression for over 30 years. I faked the smiles and I hid behind my sarcastic sense of humor. I made my way through the dark thoughts that I'd endlessly drown in. I'd curse when my alarm would ring in the morning because that meant I had to fake being alive for another day. I remember being so tired and sleep was the only thing I looked forward to. Dreaming was my reward. It was only after a separation and divorce, a re-diagnosis, a forced sick leave from my job, making the hard decision that I wasn't well enough to watch my own children, hours of introspection and meditation, feeling my suppressed emotions and coming to terms with my sabotaging ego that I am not the suffering child, teenager, and adult that I had adamantly thought I was. I had carried my entire past with me and doing so made me suffer a great deal because I didn't have the power to let it all go. I didn't know what my life would entail if I let it all go because it became my identity. The fear of even thinking about that possibility scared me into a train of incessant thoughts and kept me in a lethal state of mind.

I learned so much about myself and looked at every piece that made me. I honored myself and my truth. I honored my suffering and loved myself back to life. I loved myself so hard especially in the darkest moments of my life when I didn't think I was worthy of love. I learned that my old story was only a story and I had the power to create a new one in this present moment. It was a decision I had to consciously make despite how scary it felt. I felt like I was going to lose myself in the process, but I had gained so much more in the end when it was released without hesitation. That's when I started to heal. I remember those days of despondence. How I dreamed of a life of simplicity and beauty. I thought I could only attain it in my dreams but I can attest, from my own unique experience after all I have been through, that I am here.

Conclusion – Letting Go

"I'm not the same person I was yesterday, the day before, last week, last month, or last year. When adding up all the experiences, wisdom, knowledge, and love gained and lost along the way, today I am someone different as I will be again tomorrow." –Tena M. Dodds

I woke up one day and realized that I'd walked so far away from myself and created a life built on other's expectations, automatic programming, societal norms, and the false pretense that these decisions would lead me to happiness. What I was really doing was ignoring my own needs and cultivating a life not of my soul's desire but instead from my lack of self-worth. While focusing outwardly and trying to meet expectations, I ignored myself and what I really wanted out of life leading me into spiritual death. At this point, I didn't even know what I wanted. I didn't even know myself.

Being able to connect with my spirit guides, I thought that my purpose was to relay messages to the outside world but unfortunately, I failed to internalize those messages. The teacher must first learn the lessons. I was so busy trying to fix and help others, that I was slowly wearing down and falling deeper into a hole of discomfort and pain. I wondered why I wasn't happy but was more depressed than ever.

At that point, I knew I had let go of my old life, I had to unbecome everything that I thought I was and discover who I really am. I had to create a new life, a life centering on getting to know myself and what I really wanted. I realized that this required letting go of many things, relationships included. I had to shed many layers of the false sense of self that I had accumulated over my lifetime, all the things that didn't align with my higher self and its purpose. I was tired of living a lie.

With my new set of eyes and inspiration, I set out to make myself a priority for the first time ever. I realized that I can't help anyone until I help myself. That's what's so beautiful about the life we have: we can choose at any time to begin again with a blank canvas. So I made the decision to discover myself, what I liked and disliked, what I loved or hated, what turned me on and what made me fizzle. Without any interference from others or influence from societal norms, I started a new path, this time carved uniquely for me.

On this path, I want to let go of everything that no longer serves my highest good as a spirit inhabiting human form. I want to be my own somebody; I want to do what feels good to my soul and my divine expression in this world. I want to accept myself, flaws, imperfections, mistakes included. I want to be sure of myself, to know my worth… No fear, no doubt, no guilt, no insecurity. With every breath, in every moment, I want to love myself and be unapologetically me.

I know now that I'm not here to just preach the words but to set the example for others to follow. To embody love and acceptance and to give permission for others to do the same. To create a life of my own that I don't have to run away from and that makes me happy. To realize the truth that I've always been whole, and to live this new life with my wholeness leading the way. There is freedom waiting on the other side, the freedom that comes after the journey home to me.

Chapter 2

Authentic Self

"She is magic
When she left her conditioned life and fear behind
She decided to be real
Guided solely by the Divine light of her soul.
It was her mantra;
Her newfound truth
The truth of being free."

Karen A. Baquiran

Introduction – Authentic Self

"Your Divine Spirit deserves the most extraordinary of things. You are worthy. Don't settle for less." –Tena M. Dodds

What does change mean to you? Change can be scary as hell, especially when you're used to living a comfortable life. But sometimes, comfortable isn't the answer because it can mean that we aren't choosing what we really want and we aren't honouring our truth. It will sometimes mean that we have to make a decision that can and will alter our entire life and the lives of those involved.

I remember when I decided to leave my husband; even the thought of it scared the shit out of me. I was terrified to say it out loud because saying it would mean it was really true even though I was suffering in silence. I had to think about the ripple effect of my choices, who it would affect and the impact it would make. I barely had any self-worth at the time and I didn't think I was capable of making such a decision that included young children. Who leaves their husband when their kids are 3 and 1 year old?

I was comfortably uncomfortable in my life but I knew deep down in my soul that I wasn't happy. I knew I couldn't keep going with these shenanigans because it was exhausting me to have to keep up with the pretending and the acceptance of my reality. I was scared to finally find myself at the fork in the road of my life and having to boldly make a decision that would cause a lot of chaos in my safe and secure life.

I had to surrender my fear and be courageous for myself. I couldn't live with myself knowing that I had stayed in a marriage that wasn't allowing me to grow. I couldn't stay and teach my kids that it's okay to stay in an unhappy union and that this was love. I had to teach them that I had to follow my heart and serve myself knowing that in the long term, it would be the best decision for all of us. I had to take a chance and choose myself with the risk that everyone would judge me, dislike me, disown me. I couldn't go home another day and lie to him and falsely lead him to think I was okay when I wasn't. I couldn't ignore the cries from my soul any longer. The screams got way too loud that I did what I had to do, without a plan, it was just my truth in that moment and I couldn't look back. I had to honor myself and what my soul knew to be true.

We may never be ready for any life-altering event or choice. But I don't regret my choices because I actually felt myself breathe freedom for the first time. These kinds of feelings keep persisting within us and they continuously whisper until they get loud enough to become a roar and we are left without a choice. I can imagine how stuck people get because of the fear. I remember having to convince myself for a long time that I was crazy for even thinking of leaving because he was so good to me. I remember beating myself up and blaming myself for being unhappy and making excuses to the point that I would suck it up again and again. It's scary and I have full compassion for those that live in denial and fear, but I'm just going to leave this here if you need a sign. This is it. When you know, you just know. Courage comes when you can take that leap of blind faith and jump knowing very well that you are serving your highest good and trusting that everything is going to be alright.

2.1 Authentic Self

"The only person we should depend on to make us feel valuable is our self. It doesn't matter how often others tell us how wonderful we are if we don't believe it, if we don't believe in ourselves. It's become such a habit for us to sabotage with negative self-talk that we don't realize what we're doing. We should speak to ourselves with patience, kindness, and compassion as if we were speaking to a lover, child, or best friend. Once we change how we silently speak to ourselves, we can watch the magic of truly loving ourselves unfold." –Tena M. Dodds

I've noticed a problem within myself and it took a bit of time to realize because it just seemed normal to me. Sometimes when we think something is normal, we could actually be in a danger zone because we don't even realize the harm we're doing. I never really gave myself credit for anything because I always felt like my existence was simply mediocre and there wasn't more to me than what I saw in the mirror. I never felt I was important or capable of doing anything good and I would continuously downplay any successful situation with phrases like "I was probably lucky" or "Yes, we'll see if it works out next time" or "I know! Who would have thought that I could do that?"

Negative self-talk seems to be part of my everyday vocabulary but now that it's been brought into my awareness, the challenge lies in thinking outside of the harsh self-criticism. I need to see myself the way people who love me, see me. I need to see and accept every reason why they love me. The next chapter of my life is truly recovering from not loving myself enough and to see that I am complete as I am. I've learned that no matter how damaged one thinks they are, it is simply a matter of opinion and self-judgment. We are always whole just as we are in this moment.

I looked at myself today in the mirror after a long day at work and I saw myself in a different light. I'm a natural observer and I usually look straight at the places on my face that I don't like but instead, I tried something different. I gave myself a compliment instead. "You've got nice eyes, Karen." I'll be honest, saying it kind of made me cringe and I noticed the negative self-talk that would immediately flood my mind: "Are you

sure they're nice? They're just ok. There's nothing special about them."
I shook my head as if to scold myself. I never noticed how automatic it
became for me to bring myself down. If I'm not going to love myself or see
my own worth, how can I move forward in growth when I don't have the
self-confidence to believe it's possible? I was always striving to be better and
truer to my authentic self but I never even noticed how I spoke internally.

I knew that it would take a lot of work to take control of my thoughts and
change the negative words into good ones. I've been sending bad images
of myself into the Universe for a long time and that isn't fair to me. I had
to look deep into my eyes, into the windows of my soul and listen to my
internal dialogue. I needed to rectify the situation. How can I love and
think highly of myself when I'm allowing my ego to talk negatively to my
soul? It was horrible to think that I've been in this subtle, yet damaging
verbally self-abusive relationship for this long. I can't even think of the
last time I gave myself a compliment for anything. How can I evolve to be
everything that I wanted to be if I don't feel good enough to get there? I
always felt like I didn't deserve success. I've always high-lighted my failures
and found solutions to fix them but when I would actually succeed, I never
acknowledged that I learned something.

Looking back, we can't grow and move forward when we don't complete
the lesson at hand. We will fail so many times, learn from it, and live our
newfound truth, but we should also give ourselves a pat on the back to
acknowledge our success. When we can speak to ourselves with kindness,
we are opening space for a new thought process and we no longer leave
room for negativity. This shift in perception has opened my eyes and I am
willing to give myself the nod of approval.

We all want to be somebody, but I have truly failed at looking at the simpler
picture. I am somebody within my family, friends, and acquaintances. I
am a mother, an awesome ex-wife, a girlfriend, a daughter, a sister, an aunt,
a best friend, a cousin, a niece, a colleague, a neighbor. We have certain
titles and these titles don't make us who we are but they may actually mean
something to someone. The people that surround us are a mirror to who
we are inside, so if they're able to express their gratitude for our existence

or if they're giving us genuine credit for everything we have accomplished, we should be thankful and accept their gifts of showing us our reflection through their eyes. It's so important now for me to accept their kind words and their gestures to help me see my own worth. But regardless of our titles, we are each somebody, period. Nothing else needed. We are worthy just as we are.

It's so easy for me to see the good in others and to help them become more than they thought they ever could be, so why not me? I am valuable enough to know my worth and allow my higher self to shine much more than I have ever allowed before. I have a lot of work ahead in my journey to raise myself higher because the negative self-talk all these years has truly prevented me from going the whole way through. A lot of my challenges and defeats may have been learned but they aren't truly completed because I hindered the impact of the lesson upon my growth.

What I know for sure is that I am a good person. From acknowledging this simple truth, I can finally allow myself to believe that I deserve great things in my life. I have a beautiful gift of expression and composing life lessons that may touch someone else's life and may help them in their own journey to worthiness. Now that I am consciously aware of the way I would speak to myself, it's time for me to turn those negative words into positive ones. It's time for me to give myself the credit for all that I have ever done. My life is mine and I cannot lead by example if I'm not applying my words to my own life and creating them into actions. My recovery from negative self-talk and work towards knowing my worth is a process but I am willing to own up to my life and know that whatever lies ahead will be part of my beautiful journey.

2.2 Authentic Self

"As a society we've been taught to constantly look outside ourselves to fill a void within, but it's only when we realize that all the answers live inside us that we are truly free." –Tena M. Dodds

What do you want out of life? A big house? A luxury car? Lots of money? To retire? A 5-Star vacation? Diamonds? Everything top of the line? It seems we are always buying stuff to fill a void and we think these things will make us happy. But these things only give us temporary gratification and then we're already looking for our next quick fix on the never-ending quest for *satisfaction*. If we're always buying things in the search for happiness, we're neglecting the important values that actually satisfy our souls.

We are trained very early on by society to look to material goods to make us feel good, to make us feel worthy. We're always trying to one-up our neighbor or impress our friends and family with the idea that having things equals success. Yes, we all want and deserve to be financially abundant. Who doesn't want that kind of freedom? But we tend to think money will solve ALL our problems. It does to a certain point, but then what about the meaningful things that money can't buy?

When we stop looking at material things to make us content, we should acknowledge the things in life that come for free and that feed the soul entirely. Connection and love is enough to comfort. Trust is enough to ease uncertainty. Faith is enough to hold us steady. It's the very basics that are enough to give us exactly what we need. No need to compete to be richer or better. People who have less find it easier to be content because they make the best of what they've got and are grateful for what they do have instead of focusing on what they don't. They thrive on the abundance of love and joy in their lives.

When we're stripped bare of all the material things, labels, titles, statuses that we think make us who we are, we are left with only the essence of who we are at the core of our being. The question is, would you be happy with that person? At the very core of every human being lies a deep well of unconditional love that can be tapped into at any given moment. This love can and will carry us forward and fill us up with more than we'll ever need. It offers us much more than anything we could fit inside a big house.

If we look to the material world and things outside of ourselves to make us happy, then we'll always be drowning, hoping to fill the internal gap. The thing that people don't realize is that this gap will only get larger and wider and deeper until we find ourselves in a deep dark abyss of nothingness. So, it's imperative to realize that things don't equal happiness. We are already worthy, complete, enough, and whole at the core of our being because that being is love, and our bank richness will never amount to the richness of love.

2.3 Authentic Self

"Happiness is being the most authentic version of yourself, doing what's true for your soul." –Tena M. Dodds

When we walk the world with an open mind and heart, we are able to love easily. When we're confidently walking in love, the pain seems less and anger, distant. The colors appear brighter and we will see life as simply beautiful. We are no longer searching because we know we already have the answers inside. We find it easy to quiet our minds from all the noise that fills our everyday lives so that we can truly listen to our inner being. Anything negative that comes up will be dealt with in a calm and non-dramatic manner. Our feelings get hurt less often and we are content and grateful for what the Universe brings into our lives. Love acts as a shield against negativity and our minds are in control of this love shield.

I know this makes it seem easy and some of us may be so far from this kind of reality but it's definitely achievable. It's a matter of thinking positive and training and rewiring our brains to replace negative thought patterns. One thought at a time, day by day, putting in the effort to leave behind old beliefs and thought patterns of self-doubt, fear, worry, and self-sabotage. We need to acknowledge what we bring to the table and love the person that we are right now in this moment. Each and every one of us is enough exactly as we are, and it's from that state of feeling like we are enough that real lasting change is made.

We need to be more accepting of the idea that we deserve love just as much as anyone else. When opportunity arises, we can replenish our souls with love's healing powers. And when we feel full, we naturally pay that love forward to others.

We are stronger than we give ourselves credit for. I can look back at the days when I would sleep hours on end because I felt like there was not enough of a reason to get up and live. I decided one day to gradually do a bit of mental rearranging and to push through the barriers that kept me small. I pushed my hoarded insecurities aside and looked deep within my being. I found my hope and I took it out and decided to hold onto it. We all have the choice to make our lives better or stay where we are. There is love within each of us waiting to be found.

2.4 Authentic Self

"Many of us follow the life path set out before us by others without questioning what we really want out of life and without reflecting on our heart's true desires. But at some point, it's important to start asking those questions of ourselves. Have trust in the voice of the heart and know that it will never lead you astray." –Tena M. Dodds

We can do what we want to do and be who we want to be, as long as we have trust in the journey towards our goals. A goal can be anything from finding love, getting the dream job or perfect relationships, etc. But sometimes our choices are manipulated by others, by society, family, or religion and we do things to avoid being judged. It seems that most of us would rather look for validation from others instead of asking ourselves "What do I want for my life?"

I know my older sister Carla didn't decide what career path to take because my parents *suggested* it to her. Thankfully she's capable enough to do a fantastic job and she has enough drive to go above and beyond. After all her hard work and dedication, she has reached the top in her career. But I wonder sometimes, what career path would she have chosen if she were given the opportunity to decide that on her own? How would her life be had she been given the opportunity to make her own choices and not what our parents had suggested? I am most certain she would have succeeded, regardless, but how different would her life be had she been given the opportunity to decide for herself? Maybe one day she will drop everything that she worked so hard for and actually do what she was meant to do. Maybe her real destiny will awaken and she will trust herself enough to follow it.

It's never too late to have faith in something and I think faith should start with the self. Having faith in ourselves, learning to love, and trusting our own instincts would help shape the life we are meant to live as our truest self. Whether our choices bring us towards success or failure, it's so important to do what we truly want with the intention of following our heart instead of fulfilling the expectations of others.

We shouldn't point our fingers and blame others for forcing us to make our decisions. We always have the last say if it has to do with our life. I've heard it many times when people would say, "They made me choose it because if I didn't, then there would be a conflict." People will always have an opinion and it's nice if we have someone whose opinion we value. But after all contemplation and tallying of opinions, we should take the time to ask ourselves: are we happy with the choice? Are we ok to take that risk or that leap of faith? Would we rather make our own mistakes than have to argue our way with someone who wants to dictate our lives? Are we ok with failure? Is failure so bad or is it a necessary part of life? What's holding us back from doing what we really want? We should try to understand that yes, failure does suck, but failure is inevitable and necessary. It is there to test us, to teach us something, and to better who we are because without it, we would never know what real success tastes like.

I encourage everyone to dream a little and to ask, "What is my life's dream? What does my heart desire? What is my purpose?" And without thinking of judgment from others, we should also ask ourselves, "What do I want for myself? Is it attainable?" I really believe that anything is attainable if we put ourselves out there and if we try to get over that barrier of fear of failure. It doesn't matter how long it takes because the real joy is in the adventure rather than the end goal. I would rather reach for my dreams and fail than wonder what if? Having faith will take us a long way towards our authentic life path, faith in ourselves, and faith that we are loved and supported by all that is Divine. Our life deserves its own signature, even if people don't approve.

2.5 Authentic Self

"Listening to your intuition is the key to self mastery." –Tena M. Dodds

I'm sure we've all said at least once in our lives, "I should have listened to my instincts!" And yes, we should have! We all should listen to our intuition. It's our internal guidance system and we all have one. It's a guide, an inner voice, a gut feeling, a knowing that speaks to us when we need it most and listening to it takes practice, patience, and awareness. The driver of our thoughts has been programmed at an early age by a voice that doesn't always serve our highest good. That voice within our mind (our ego) can instill fear, insecurity, doubt, uncertainty, and can keep us in an anxious state of being. This voice within us wants to keep us safe and protect us, but what happens to us when we live in a state of fear? Does that give us room to grow? Does it give us the opportunity to see what's outside the box and see that we are only limited by what we are scared to experience?

Our intuition speaks to us when we contemplate decisions, feelings, plans etc. and the choice is always ours whether we listen and follow through but we sometimes mistake our egoic thoughts for truth. We then learn the hard way and know deep down that in hindsight, we should've listened to our inner voice. The ego will always give us a reason for why we shouldn't do things. It's too risky. You're going to make a mistake. You will be humiliated. What if you fail? Whereas, our intuition will tell you to forget fear and do it anyway. How can we become a sovereign being if we will not stand in our truth and passion?

What is it that distracts us from our truth? Firstly, not trusting ourselves and what we know is right. Secondly, the role of other people's thoughts and opinions will influence us. And thirdly, the media plays a role by infiltrating our psyche with what they believe is socially acceptable, therefore, influencing our own personal thoughts and decisions. We're being bombarded by noise in all directions and in turn, we fail to listen to our truth. In the grander scheme of things, we are being hindered by the egos of everything external to our own inner voice, therefore we become stuck between who we are told to be and who we have the potential to become.

Meditation is a great practice to embrace stillness and presence in this now moment. It is a useful tool to not necessarily quiet the mind, but to calm it and simply allow the thoughts to come and pass without judgment to what one sees or feels. If we can learn to calm the mind from going a mile a minute and slow down the noise from distracting our inner being, the guiding voice can openly come forth. I used to meditate when it came time for decision making. It was the only time I could contemplate without judgment. And like any practice, doing this has allowed my inner voice to become my inner compass in what feels right in my now moment. I've learned to trust myself through my journey, to not beat myself up if it doesn't go right, but to simply embrace that it was meant for me and I am here to learn lessons that will sharpen my inner voice for future references. I will not be guided by fear, but I will be responsibly cautious when I take any leap forward.

There are times we feel that we want to express our truth without fear of being rejected or judged, and we end up keeping our precious hopes and dreams locked away in the cabinet. Some of us would rather live in a state of self-scrutiny, as our ego keeps us in check, keeps us safe and secure because the feeling of rejection is far greater than the risk of taking the leap for what our soul desires.

Our instincts are what guide us through life. With awareness alone, they can direct us through scenarios that require a decision. We should allow them to guide us and if we feel that our gut told us the wrong thing, was it really that wrong? Take the good with it and see it as a lesson. Everything life throws at us is a lesson to be learned and happens for the very purpose of our own individual growth.

By calming the mind, we don't have to depend on our ego to lead our life. Instead, we can choose to go with what our guiding voice tells us and we'll know when a choice feels right and when it doesn't. It speaks to us louder if we just pay the slightest bit of attention. It is a feeling that cannot be ignored as it is the soul speaking to our highest possible outcome. The voice will never leave us and one day when we learn to listen to it over the chatter of our thoughts, we will see that we're not crazy, but lucky that our inner voice has been there the entire time.

2.6 Authentic Self

"Set yourself free from the routine, try something new, do something different for a change and see where it takes you. Life is a grand adventure or a boring collection of decisions. You always get to choose." –Tena M. Dodds

Many of us have a daily routine that keeps us comfortable but that comfortability soon brings us to a plateau in our growth. The routine then becomes our life and when we get off-track, or something goes wrong, we feel frustrated that our day isn't going as planned. Sound a bit familiar? To a certain extent, we are obsessed with having control over our situations as much as possible because let's face it, the majority of people would rather live comfortable lives than be hitting curveballs all the time. But let's say, we said, *"Screw control for today and let's see what happens..."* How would the day be? How would we feel about this?

Every action is a choice we make. By always trying to comfort ourselves by doing things that we can predict, we never prepare ourselves for things that may go off-track. For those who are bold enough, I challenge you to do something different in your day. You can call out from work, or not make your morning coffee, or take a different route entirely. Little things can make a big difference. Shake it up a bit!

The choice is ours whether we want to shine brightly or not and the potential of daring to be different lies in every single one of us. We need to stop doubting our passions and our ability to try new things if it means broadening our horizons and doing something out of the ordinary. It keeps life exciting and makes a difference. We need to believe in the possibilities, believe in ourselves, and believe in our dreams. There's no harm in trying before we decide that we're incapable.

Life will pass us by quickly if we choose not to fulfill our dreams. Some of us don't even know what our purpose is in life but we can try to find what inspires and motivates us and start from there. We can choose adventure over routine and make everything we do count. A lot of us are trained to live life like a herd of sheep, blindly following along without asking any vital questions that could change the course of our journey. And when it comes to the end of our lives, we end up dying with regrets and an untouched bucket list. We end up dying not fulfilling our missions and thinking we could have done more. We see these kinds of tragedies happen every day and we end up proclaiming, "Screw it, life is short…" but the follow through becomes short lived.

We forget and we go back to comfort and practicality. I would rarely choose what I wanted, because I always wanted to serve and please others around me. It took a while for me to ask myself what I wanted out of my own life and slowly I played dare with myself and chose a different direction. If I had not chosen anything for my own highest good, I never would have done the things I thought were impossible. I never would have taken that road trip, mended my broken heart and trusted that the great love was potentially out there. I never would have found my soul and bonded over forgotten dreams. I never would have walked alongside the inner magic I had once forgotten, and fallen so in love with the discovery of who I am.

2.7 Authentic Self

"Authenticity is not about being fearless, but about showing up despite the fear of rejection, in the truest, most vulnerable embodiment of you in that moment. It's about being real and true to your soul. It's about honesty and it's a choice to be seen for who you really are. Because to be who you truly are, is the greatest gift you can give yourself as well as those around you." –Tena M. Dodds

I've met a lot of people and have observed a lot in researching human behavior. I noticed that a lot of people can go through waves of authenticity or they're selective in who they can be real with. Sometimes pressure from outside sources such as society, family, or friends, manipulates a person into believing that they're something that they're not.

We can easily feel insecure for fear of rejection. There is a problem with the world if we're not teaching our children that it's okay to be who they truly are and that it doesn't matter what anyone else thinks. We need to foster in them enough self-confidence and self-worth by teaching them about self-love in order to better handle judgment from peers. By teaching them to accept everyone for who they are and to stop criticizing what's considered different, we allow for them to not only accept themselves, but others as well.

If there was no such thing as judgment, how different would our world be? People would be more inclined to be their true selves. Confidence would be easier to build and acceptance would be everywhere. Realistically, we know that this would never diminish 100%, but if we carry ourselves in this truth, we can start a ripple effect. With compassion, empathy, and our own authenticity, we can be the guiding light, giving others a sense of security and safety to be themselves as well.

2.8 Authentic Self

"The greatest people in history sometimes had hundreds of failures before their ultimate success. It's better to start something and fail than to never try at all." –Tena M. Dodds

I love hearing stories about people who follow their dreams and reach their goals and I especially love hearing the end of the story when they say, "I did it at 126 years old! Can you believe it?" It is never too late to follow our dreams. We will always have an excuse as to why we can't do something but if our hearts continue to seek and wonder, a curiosity will emerge and light a fire inside of us that needs to be discovered and released.

I have always wanted to be a writer but my lack of confidence due to criticism was always a reason to not pursue a career. I always thought that where I lived also played a huge role in not succeeding. Life then gets in the way. I found a job that I love to do but it doesn't compare to how free it makes me feel to write. There will always be obstacles and we sometimes choose to side with excuses over what we truly desire. Whether we like it or not, there will always be something in our way. There is no right time; the only time is now. The shift in thinking to choose our heart's desire over excuses is the biggest obstacle of them all.

I always find myself in the fast lane wondering when my breakthrough will happen. I know that there's a possibility that it may never happen but I choose to believe that it will. A realist may say I'm being naïve and delusional. The pessimist may say that my dreams won't pay the bills. But the dreamer may encourage me to do what I love despite the outcome. Looking too far into an unpredictable future is what takes away from the experience. It is what kills the spark of joy and potential outcome of what if. Sometimes I think people can be too strong with their opinions, but I know that they are only projecting their own limitations onto me. It doesn't mean that I am not going to try just for the sake of experiencing it, despite what they say. I am not looking for a massive pay out, I'm looking to let my soul experience itself.

We should believe in ourselves, have the courage to see our potential, and try to make something of our lives even if nothing comes from it. It doesn't matter what it is, just deciding that we want to give ourselves a chance is the biggest decision to change our lives. If everyone were to take the time to focus on what makes them happy, we can imagine the kind of world we'd live in. We can do anything we want to do, if we have that drive within us. It requires strength and bravery to push past our perceived limitations and know that it's never too late to follow our dreams. It's better to start something than to never try at all.

2.9 Authentic Self

"Wisdom is only healed pain." –Tena M. Dodds

Often we can unjustly assume that our quality of life is less than ideal if we put our focus on what's going wrong instead of what's going right. But sometimes we figure it out when we're put in a difficult situation that makes us deeply reflect on our lives. We're responsible for trudging forward and making our experiences as meaningful as possible. I can remember being so consumed by my pain that I became a victim, but it took one huge relapse in depression to make me see the light within my suffering.

We find ourselves asking, what is the point of all this pain? Why am I suffering much more than everyone else? When will this end? But there is a master plan for everything. Sometimes people take a ton of hits in life but what's amazing is how they still find the strength to get up every morning. Perhaps some days are harder than others, but it's a miracle that they can actually find the strength to continue and fight for the quality of their life.

We can all look back on when we've conquered those painful moments and see the emotional scarring it's caused. And although some days are much more difficult than others, we're not usually given anything that we can't handle. It's okay to give ourselves credit when we're in midst of this pain and actually say, "I'm still here and I'm going to fight for myself." Whether we like it or not, we're the master creators of our reality and in charge of the way we handle our issues. If we want to be happy, we have to choose to be happy. We cannot remain a victim of the old stories that keep us feeling small and disempowered.

Most of the time we have zero control over what happens to us, but we have 100% control with how it makes us feel and how we respond. I'm not saying that it's not okay to feel sad or angry when it's appropriate; I'm saying it's not okay to remain there and hold a grudge for the long haul. We have to make the decision to accept ourselves for who we are in this now moment, that whatever happened in the past may be long gone and we are no longer going to allow it to hold us back in our pursuit of self-love and happiness. It takes a lot of courage to let go of our old stories because then we actually have to take accountability for how we carry ourselves in the world despite the haunting of old ghost stories. I will not shame myself for the pain I have felt, but instead, when the layers are peeled off, I can celebrate my survival and what it took to get there.

2.10 Authentic Self

"We seem to be always waiting for a miracle, unaware that the miracle is life itself." –Tena M. Dodds

I've experienced many groundhog days, where my daily routine was as predictable as any Hollywood ending, except my life wasn't anywhere close to being Hollywood. My life was a mundane scene, day in and day out. I'd wake to the same morning alarm and leave while it was still dark. I'd see the same houses as I'd walk to the metro. The only change of scene was the natural evolution of the four seasons, but I was the same as I walked those quiet streets. I had accepted that nothing was going to change for me and I didn't think I had the capability of doing a thing about it. I felt like I didn't know how to even begin to change and I didn't have the courage to do anything drastic. I had done everything the same for years and felt completely stuck and hating my routine. My mind kept wandering away from my present day and just that screamed red flags.

I would think a lot on my walks, making plans for my work-life, my personal life, and my goals. Thinking like this all the time started to slowly change my perception. And in that change of perception came a new way of viewing everything around me. I felt like I was able to take that time to make decisions and feel good about them. Those walks were motivating me to get out of the dead end and out of my head. I wasn't happy anymore at my job. I didn't feel like I was getting anywhere over there. The environment was getting too toxic and instead of it being my safe haven, it was turning into another place I wanted to avoid.

I was walking home one day and pondering my job that I said out loud, "I will even go to another hospital even if I can't speak the language." I surrendered to those words. Within days, I got a call from an old colleague who told me they were looking for new workers at the new hospital. I hesitated because for the first time, I declared something and it manifested quickly. I had to really think fast because those job postings were going really quick but instead of feeling excitement, I also felt fear. Everything I was insecure about myself came to the forefront and I felt like I had lost myself in that safe routine and now I actually had to do something about it. And of course this new job opportunity was at the French hospital and I had no idea how to speak French. But I asked for it! I was very specific about what I asked for and there it was, a real way out.

I couldn't deal with anything outside of my comfort zone but here I was and I had to make a decision. Despite my fear of change, I reflected back on the many hours I had lost just in my commute to work. I had thought of my quality of life and how I desperately wanted a healthier work environment. I kept looking for an opportunity and here it was. The decision was easy. I applied for the job and practiced everyday speaking French to prepare for my interview. I ended up getting the job when I completely surrendered. I left it up to the ether to work its magic because by this time I had zero control and I was excited. Walking to work while I waited for the call back was different because I was just proud that I stepped up for myself and I wanted to savor that.

Looking back, I had spent so much time with my head down, counting steps and getting lost in my thoughts. Being out of that routine, I was able to see how incredible that journey was. It surely didn't feel like it at the time. I really felt like I was losing myself when in fact it was the Universe stirring my reality so that I snap out of it and take that leap of change. Life can really feel limiting when we put our focus on our misery. But what I'm so proud of was that I declared my readiness and jumped at the opportunity when it presented itself in that magical manifested moment. I could have easily remained in that safe place and eventually lost myself in that routine, but I knew in every second of that dead end routine that there was more out there for me.

2.11 Authentic Self

"We spend way too much time worrying what people will think of us when the truth is they barely think of us at all. When they do, it's only to boast their opinion of which has no bearing on our life anyway. The only person we need to impress is our own self. When we truly don't care what anyone thinks of us, we come dangerously close to our own personal freedom." —Tena M. Dodds

It was always a desire of mine to be understood. I'm really not a complicated person but I've always felt an emotional disconnect between what I classified as "regular folk" and myself. I was always interested in people's stories because underneath their story lies a puzzle piece of who they really are. What I learned at a young age is that people want to be seen and heard, however there is a part of them that likes to run away from that truth because the thought of being seen can be too painful. I always felt like I had a gift in bridging their pain with reality, giving them the safety to reveal their deepest, darkest secrets, but I know from experience that people mostly don't like being mirrored and they sometimes can't bear to see themselves out of guilt or shame.

For the longest time I tried to fake social cues and bring myself to a level of being falsely understood. I figured, if people can't give themselves to me after I tried to go deep, then how else can I open up on a level where they won't run from me? I knew on a deeper level that this wasn't what I had been searching for, and when you feel rejected so often, you end up thinking there must be something wrong with you. It was a way to feel validated and part of the crowd because I never took the time to validate myself. What I learned is that it was never about me at all. I eventually gave up pretending because it was too exhausting to be something I didn't resonate with. It was too exhausting to wear a mask just to fit in with people who didn't appreciate me. I accepted that I couldn't be fully understood and it was okay to remain alone if it meant that I wouldn't compromise the integrity of who I am.

What I know today is that staying true to who I am is not a bad thing, but should be encouraged. My sister has said that I should stop looking at myself like I am unlovable but I should embrace that I am unconventional and unique. When we're comfortable with who we are in our true authenticity, we can be that person at every step of the way because there is no more pretending. It's just who we are. When we can accept this and truly open our hearts to loving and accepting ourselves fully, then we can open our hearts to love and accept another human being just as they are. The right people will come our way and even if they're not big in numbers, just having one good friend who accepts us fully and unconditionally is enough.

By being able to fully embrace who we are, we will attract our own tribe. The people who we attract will love us, accept us, and not judge us. They are the rare people who will listen to our stories, hear and see us for who we are, love us even when we feel we aren't worthy and make us feel like we matter. These rare connections don't happen so often but when they do, sometimes they unlock the doors within us that we are too afraid to open. In the end, I feared rejection, but when I chose to fully accept myself, there was no more fear. It made it a lot easier to open up and give myself because of the knowingness that my true self and the mysteries of my past were accepted, loved, and safe with those who made the effort to know me.

2.12 Authentic Self

"The Universe speaks to us through magic, it's all around us all the time in the whispering of the trees, the rustling of the leaves, the beating of your heart and the birds and the bees. You only need to open your eyes enough to see." —Tena M. Dodds

At a young age, my grandfather introduced me to magic. I never doubted for a second that what I saw was real and happening for me. Everyday there was a show, a sign from some Divine Source. Everyday was magical for me until I had to grow up and was forced out of Neverland. I never thought that the signs I'd been searching for when I was an adult were the same type of magic I manifested as a child. I had forgotten how it felt to receive validating messages when I was contemplating decisions and not knowing if I should trust what I was feeling deep down or resist the change out of fear.

Signs and synchronicities from the Universe can appear anywhere and everywhere. They can show up as musical lyrics, a feather on the grass, pennies from the sky, seeing the same sequence of numbers on license plates and the clock, seeing a specific bird or butterfly, etc. Signs from the Universe can be anything that resonate deeply within the soul and that we apply meaning to. They come to validate when we're on the right track and to inspire us to keep going. It's real magic! I can remember thinking that everything was way too coincidental to not be a sign. Of course the skeptic in me needed more signs 'cause let's face it, our view of magic gets tainted at a young age. Santa Claus isn't real, the Tooth Fairy is your mom, and those magic tricks "you saw" only happened when they told you to close your eyes.

I realized that we can easily forget what we once believed with conviction. We were once fearless and believed so wholeheartedly in magic to be true even without any evidence or proof. And how is it that as children we were able to see without blinders, that it didn't matter how it happened, but that we witnessed something so profound it made us believe so deeply?

What is it that happens to us that tarnishes our view of life? I had forgotten so easily who I really was, deep down, the innocence of life, re-lived through the eyes of my children. And that joy in their faces when they witness magic sparks up the same vibrant memories that bring me back to the age when I was once a firm believer. I've witnessed magic when I could barely get out of bed. And when I asked for a sign, it was delivered every time. I've found feathers on my bathroom floor in the middle of winter. I heard songs on the radio that haven't been played in decades. These are everyday finds and these finds came up so often that I found myself to be a believer again. Maybe that was the sign after all. It was showing me to find that childlike part of me that once looked for magic everywhere. We can easily get so lost in life and put fear in the driver's seat of our destiny, but I deeply feel that if we can so boldly remember the memories of how we once felt, innocent, carefree, and full of life, then we can finally come home to who we really are.

Conclusion – Authentic Self

"You are beautiful. You are amazing. You are more than enough even if you don't get out of bed today. You don't need a big shot career, immaculately kept house, or a perfectly put-together look to be worthy of this life, to be worthy of love. You are whole and complete just as you are." –Tena M. Dodds

To be authentic requires us to be vulnerable and honest, to drop the masks and embrace all of our messy parts; parts that we feel are unworthy to be seen. We begin with a blank slate as children, expressing ourselves without the filters of world influence, and slowly the voices of those around us shame us for being who we are. This shaming voice infiltrates our psyche and ends up becoming our own inner voice. This voice inhibits our potential growth and makes us smaller and smaller as we crawl into a shell of lost identity. We get inundated with so many ideas of what it looks like to be socially accepted. We are trained from birth to act a certain way, to follow a certain religion, culture and customs, wear the right clothes, have the appropriate friends, and abide by unspoken life rules in order to avoid scrutiny from our peers.

We get to choose very little for ourselves because we're told what to do, what jobs are acceptable, that we need to find love and get married, buy a house and make babies so that they can get programmed into the same robotic citizens that we've become. We learn that anything outside the box is unacceptable, weird, crazy and that it's okay to judge because it looks different than the norm. But society's version of the norm is so far from where we need to be as the human race. We get deep into this conditioning of thoughts and beliefs that aren't even ours to begin with. They were given to us, sometimes forcefully, and within it we lose our sense of self and authenticity. We put on masks for every occasion revealing tired face after tired face, tired from pretending to be perfect and keeping up with appearances not knowing who we truly are inside.

It's scary to think that so many of us are afraid to express our true nature when we are all Divine individuals, expressing ourselves with the gift of free-will. That means, we have the freedom to do anything we dare to do, and be anything we dare to be, but somehow, we're kept imprisoned by the fear that we will not be accepted or loved for our authentic self. We can get so lost and carried away with these false stories of who we are that the moment we finally get the chance to openly be ourselves, no one in our inner circles would recognize us. Some of these programs and ways of thinking become so deeply ingrained that our self worth gets compromised and is long lost with the rest of our personality.

If we pushed for acceptance and gave the freedom of choice to everyone around, we'd probably see so many individuals come out embodying their real self without fear of rejection. Love is the only thing that can heal this deep-seated wound within us. And coming out of the authentic closet is something that most have yet to do. It took me a long time to figure myself out again after my separation and divorce. I spent a lot of time serving those around me and forgetting to take care of myself. It took a 45 minute pause in the vegetable aisle at the grocery store to make me realize that I had no idea who I was or what I really wanted because I learned so early that you just deal, and you like everything, and you can't be picky. I had not set up any standards for myself and it reflected on the relationships I made, but especially on the relationship I had with myself.

I've found it to be crucial to choose myself every single day because that is the example I had to be for my children. I didn't want them to feel ashamed for the way they express themselves and I didn't want them to learn that losing yourself along the way was the only way to be loved. It has been a journey of self discovery, sometimes frustrating and other days fun because I'm finally allowing myself to unfold as the moments go by and am remembering the true essence of who I've always been.

The soul knows what it wants, but the false inner voice becomes the dominant dictator of how the sequence of events unfolds. It's a matter of re-training the real voice of who you are to come forward and regain its place. It's the look of marvel in the eyes of my children as they discover themselves at the same time as me. It's the beautiful uncovering of my own inner world, held tightly within my soul. I've peeled back so many layers of myself, and reintroduced myself to those that thought they had known me. The people who love you no matter what will always find a place in your battleground, whereas the ones who no longer fit your mold, will fall away without apology.

It has been a brave discovery of who I am and the freedom that comes with being real is the greatest gift I've ever given myself. I no longer feel the pressure to perform because I know I am enough. I've become so aware of the voices that once told me who I was and it's changed the way I speak to my kids because I want them to only know love and not shame. I have the power to break the cycle of molding them into who I think they should be, and instead instill a safe space for them to blossom into who they already are. I had to remember that I am already whole and it doesn't take another individual to complete me. It takes a lot of courage to stand in my own sovereign self, while being surrounded by those wearing their tight-fitted masks, unbeknownst to them that they could be free like me.

Chapter 3

Presence

"Her mind kept her away,
Lost in thoughts and dreams.
She lived in a world in which she didn't belong.
But one day she had awoken
After decades of sleepwalking
And realized that all she ever had
Was this very moment.
And in an instant, her mind became one with her body
Within a life she was now mindful of."

Karen A. Baquiran

Introduction – Presence

"Courage is when we venture into the unknown despite our fearfulness, doubt, or worries and take a step anyway, having faith that the Universe always has our back." –Tena M. Dodds

I've lived so many years thinking and anticipating future events and reminiscing about puzzle pieces of vague past memories because I wasn't living in the present moment. When I surrendered to the unknown, I became aware that I had control over where I put my attention. I didn't understand why I had very little past memories and then I had an epiphany one time when I arrived at a party. The second I walked in the door, I was already anticipating and imagining myself leaving. I kept my attention thinking of a future event, probably because I was riddled with social anxiety and it was my way of control. Thinking about leaving took my attention away from what was happening right in front of me and it dawned on me as to why I had very limited memories of the past. I was physically here, but I was mentally checking out any chance I felt I had no control.

Getting out of that mental prison has given me the opportunity to be here right now. It takes a load of self awareness to listen to your own internal dialogue and realize where you're actually placing your attention. It's so refreshing to not be clouded by my thoughts anymore, but to actually be present without distraction. We are never fully certain where our lives will go, who we will meet along the way, and how our lives may or may not change. I never knew that I would be where I am today and I learned that my predictions and anticipations seldom came true.

A lot has changed for me in the last 6 years of my life and I couldn't have predicted this current state of being because of the continuous evolution of who I am. Out of the limitless potentials that can occur, we cannot predict the one outcome. Our quality of life diminishes when we obsess over control and sometimes we don't even realize we're doing it. It takes away from the mystery of life and the possibilities of the unknown and it takes courage to give it up. I realize that even when I felt afraid of change, it happened regardless so I learned to accept it despite my old patterns of hesitation.

Embracing change and living in our now moment by fully allowing it to be part of our daily journey is the key to a smooth transition into the unknown. Whatever is to come for my life, I welcome it with open arms even if there may be epic fails along the way. Whatever is to happen will happen regardless of my worries. That's the beauty of the unknown. Even if we are meant to jump left and we choose to jump right instead, the outcome has already been part of the master plan. Surrendering to what is out of our hands allows life to unfold gracefully. It takes time to re-train our thoughts because it can be scary to let go of control. By welcoming change, we can practice and commit to blindly trusting what is to come as long as we openly embrace and accept the here and now as it is.

3.1 Presence

"Life can be turbulent at times, for some more than others. Sometimes all you can do is stop thinking, worrying, stressing, or wondering about what will happen and instead have faith that it will all work out in Divine timing. Miracles happen for those who believe." –Tena M. Dodds

We all hope to live a happy life that includes a happy ending but what we fail to see is that life is a continuous journey that needs to be nurtured at every turn. When we're in a bad place, we have options. We either choose to feel sorry for ourselves or we choose to accept it. We may not know what to do during these hard times because in the moment, it's difficult to get ourselves out of it. Most of us don't know how to cope with our painful emotions and when we're deep in our feelings, the last thing we want to do is to feel anything but our suffering. What we can do to cope is observe our thoughts, acknowledge what we feel and validate it, not play into our story-telling, but to bring our attention back to our breath which then channels our inner peace. When we focus on our breath, we are ceasing the thought process. In that case, there is no suffering.

When we have faith, we know without doubt that in time we'll be able to find the strength within us to move forward. It helps to be patient in this moment and not look too far ahead. Sometimes, we can only see the big picture in hindsight, when we've moved on and learned the lesson. Looking too far ahead can make us miss important details that are happening right now. These are the crucial details that give meaning to our lives and make sense of what we're going through.

When we find ourselves fast forwarding and making endless plans, we lose track of what happens right now. And we may be pulling our attention away from everyday life's precious moments and people who are important to us. It's nice to have goals and dreams but we shouldn't dwell on something that has yet to come to fruition. We can hold that thought and desire in the moment but proceed to physically and mentally be where we are without losing ourselves.

I've taken many steps upward and I know that I'm valuable to the people who love me. I exclusively permit myself to be happy and I choose to live my life in the present moment. I have faith that every step I take will lead me exactly where I'm meant to be and if I get stuck in a bad place, I know it's only temporary and that easily takes me out of my mind. I hold a knowing that I will be strong enough to fight the fight and learn the lessons that come my way. I have enough trust in my own personal power and potential and I know that I have all the tools to help me rise above and conquer all.

I wish the same for everyone. Life can be challenging, and it's up to us not to dwell on the past or focus too much on the future but to simply remain in the present moment. We can make ourselves more aware of the negative thoughts that seep through our minds and instead of giving them power, replace them with positive ones and make it a way of life.

3.2 Presence

"If you need an example of how to live in the present moment, you need only to look to small children, animals, and all that exists in nature. There is no worry about the past or future, but only what IS right now. The tree doesn't stress over its leaves changing, it knows how to just BE in the moment and let dead things go. Let them and all of creation be your greatest teachers." –Tena M. Dodds

No matter what happens, life goes on, and as it moves forward, we have a choice to make... To remain in the past, walk along with life in the present, or run ahead envisioning the future. A lot of the time we live in the past because there are some lessons that take a little longer to learn. And although our physical body is here continuing to do things, our mind determines where we are in real time.

In my own experience before I went through my spiritual awakening, I couldn't recall many things. I can't even recall the most important events of my life, like my marriage and memories of my first child as an infant. My mind wasn't present to witness and make memories of these events. I'm not saying I completely forgot, but the memories feel vague and blurry. It's unfortunate that I'm unable to remember because I will never get back these times. I can only relive them through photos but empty holes remain. My girlfriend always tells me to be present every time I go out and I find it quite endearing because it's almost as profound as saying, "I love you."

Today, I make it a point to be one in mind and body so that I can remember the everyday moments of magic that I used to miss out on. My babies approach special milestones almost everyday and now that I have my second child, I'm awake and aware enough to hold onto those memories. We see our children and we tend to envision how their lives are going to turn out and we make plans for them as they grow up. Every parent says to a new mother and father: "Enjoy this time, it goes by so fast." And it really does, which is why we need to make the effort to be here, not only physically, but mentally and emotionally. It's a miracle to witness their development, moment to moment, each stage unique and different from the next.

Children learn by example, so we should be the best example for them to model. Or better yet, we should model our children's way of being because they're the best teachers of living presently. Children are constantly living moment to moment, they're not worried about the past nor fretting over the future. They focus their energy on what's happening in front of them and because of this, they're exceptional examples of simply being in the here and now and we should be more like them.

3.3 Presence

"Each day brings with it an opportunity to start brand new and to live life to the fullest. Each day we get to decide who we are and what we want from life. Each day we get to write and rewrite our story." –Tena M. Dodds

I have tons of insurance. There's insurance for everything, our life, house, cars, mortgage, credit, health, and so on. My financial advisor told me I'm a rare case of being overly prepared for my age. I have a notarized will, power of attorney, and three different life insurances to secure my family's comfort for when I'm either gone or incapable of speaking for myself. I know the benefits of insurance but it makes me comfortably uncomfortable being prepared for my death and assuring my family's needs are taken care of.

Insurance is somewhat morbid. It gives peace of mind but at the same time, it's preparation for sickness or death. A lot of my money is spent on insurance but when exactly should I draw the line? Money is essential for survival and freedom, so of course we'll pay to assure that our family will survive financially without us. Insurance fills the monetary void while we are gone, but I wish there was insurance to fill the void of a hug, a kiss, a conversation, love, encouragement, peace, comfort, and all the wonderful things that my children and loved ones would get from me.

We spend a lot of time preparing for our death and that takes away the time we could spend with our loved ones in the present moment. I can think of many people who have passed away. Some have gone tragically, some from sickness, and some from old age. And what does the family have to say? "I wish we had more time." Or "I wish I told them this..." We should take the time while we're still here to connect with our loved ones. We don't want to be put in a position where we live the rest of our lives with regret or guilt, wishing we had just one more day.

People are always going to be tired, busy, lazy, or whatever the excuse, but regardless, we should spend the time that we have with the people who make life worth living. We should seize each moment and make memories to add to our legacies. Insurance is all on paper; it's just a document. We're not dead yet, so we should make the effort to live our lives to the fullest. We can't take our money with us when we die, but we can at least die knowing that we were loved, that we were needed, that we were important, that we were somebody's everything. Life can be as long or as short as we want it to be. Carpe diem, seize the day.

3.4 Presence

"In the age of social media, in some ways, we're the most connected we've ever been, and in others, we're quickly losing our connection to each other. It's hard not to get sucked in with all the new gadgets and apps and games but it's also important to remember to put down the phones in the presence of other humans, pay attention to each other, be present, and have an actual face-to-face conversation with the people that you love." –Tena M. Dodds

When we speak, do people listen? When we enter a room, are we seen? We're always putting our hearts out there, wearing it on our sleeve so to speak, and in one way or another, we're looking to be validated for our existence. Sometimes we desperately want to be seen by the people we love, but their attention is elsewhere. We all fail to pay attention to others at times and it's a vicious cycle. Slowly, the human connection is shifting towards an end in existence.

I find we are too busy being socially antisocial. We're checking our Facebook, Instagram, Twitter, Google, YouTube, Pinterest and the list goes on and on. I went to a restaurant with coworkers and we were seated next to a table of four friends. The entire night these four friends were all on their mobile devices. It's a shame that people would go and physically get together but not really be there. They're being social but on another dimension. Our physical bodies can be somewhere, but if our minds aren't present, we really aren't there.

I find it so important to make these connections whether they're grand or subtle. Even a little half second eye contact is enough to show that one has been seen. We're so stuck in this cyber land and people are being misled into thinking that life resides on a social network. What we've become is a profile, with a list of friends who we actually may or may not know on an intimate level, who also have their own profile and their own list of friends. We share our life stories by checking-in somewhere, by posting selfies and pictures, and by writing up a status to tell everyone our deepest thoughts. We tag our friends if they are with us and we can make comments and like posts as a means to connect and see someone on a cyber-level. I'm guilty of this too, as most of us are to some extent.

Even though this is the future of the next generation, it's eating away at the generations before who should know better than to get trapped in the prison of the cyber world. We're easily getting distracted and we're failing to teach our children that we can actually interact face-to-face. We aren't making matters any better by being caught up in the social media craze. The next generations are slowly becoming socially inept because they rely on communication through text and typing. Let's lead the way in showing them how to properly connect with others the old-fashioned way.

I urge everyone to look around and pay attention to those who have been social-napped by media. They are everywhere but we always have the choice to be lost online or to be mentally present in our lives. Like all things in life, everything should be done in moderation. It's so much more fulfilling to make a real memory than to have a profile remember it for us.

3.5 Presence

"Love and presence are the greatest gifts we can give someone."—Tena M. Dodds

I'm not the best mom and I will never claim to be. Sometimes I don't think I'm cut out for the job, but it's a little too late for me in that department because I have two kids. I feel like I could always improve my quality of time with them. I should be conscious enough to make the effort, particularly when I have them with me. The choice should be an obvious one but sometimes it isn't so apparent to me, especially if I'm consumed by what I'm doing. They don't ask for much, but I do know that when they desire my attention, I should give it to them.

I can think back of feeling neglected by my parents. I understand now where my parents came from because I do feel like I want to live my best life. However, it isn't fair to repeat that same cycle with my children. I do find at times that I am not present with them. I am so easily distracted and scrolling on my phone and being anywhere but here with them. I remind myself how it made me feel as a child. That I didn't want very much from my parents. I just wanted them and that was enough.

It would kill me to think I was breaking my child's heart if they felt I didn't love them. I want them to feel seen and heard because this is how their self-worth develops. This is exactly where I lost mine growing up. It's been a difficult balancing act for me to be true to myself and to be a mother. I find this will always be a work in progress, considering I'd only developed a loving relationship with myself after they were born. I've got all this excitement about life, an excitement I never thought I'd have. I feel like my soul is being pulled every which way, but I can't go for too long because I have shared custody and can't just pick up and leave.

Being an adult, I have forgiven my parents for wanting to live when we were growing up. I had so much resentment, but I get it now that I am a parent. Then I bring myself back as the child and how that affected me and it was a confusing mind-fuck. I don't want that for my children. I should make the effort every chance I get because we don't get this time back. This is a crucial time in their development and they have to see it through my actions that I am here for them and I love them. Children are so forgiving, but I don't want to reach that threshold point where there is no turning back, especially when I know better. I can always do better. We can easily get so lost in our selfish ways, but I do think the key is finding that healthy balance between what's best for me and what's best for them. My kids don't care about what I give them, what I'm doing, or where I am. They just want me when they're with me and I owe it to them and my inner child to break that unhealthy cycle.

3.6 Presence

"I will not armor myself against the world, I will no longer let my love be restricted by fear, I will remain open and vulnerable, love myself and let that love be an outward expression of my healing spirit." –Tena M. Dodds

I've been driving to work and back home at different parts of the day and when I pick up my son, he sometimes tells me to stop and look at something. Today we stopped to see a cat on the street and as we watched it do absolutely nothing, I looked around and noticed a tree that I never saw before and the sky behind it, so beautiful with the sun and the clouds. We, as a culture, rarely stop to pay attention to the world around us and because of that, we fail to appreciate the little things. Kids are more in tune with nature and their surroundings; everything is fresh and new. But as adults, we're so disconnected from ourselves and our surroundings that we don't realize the simple beauties that were there all along.

At times, we want to be seen by everyone around us but we don't have the voice to simply ask someone, "Do you see me?" If we aren't paying attention, how are we able to see who we are? We are a dying society that would rather seek love from the superficial and fill our voids with material goods instead of finding true love from the one person we are with 24/7: ourselves.

If we're searching for love from others to validate us, we may be looking in the wrong place because other people are in the same boat and they're feeding on their own emptiness. It's a chain of events that may be sufficient for the time being, but in the long run, the search lacks depth and will eventually run its course. We can only meet someone as far as we've met ourselves.

Sometimes it takes a true connection with another human to be able to look at ourselves through their perspective. They act as a mirror to who we truly are and they allow us the ability to see ourselves through them. Who we truly are is the soul underneath all the layers of conditioning and beliefs that we've accumulated throughout life. Truth be told, when we take away everything materialistic, we're stripped down to the spirit inside this physical form. Can you function knowing you have nothing left materialistically? Can you survive the harsh world as you know it? Do you love yourself enough to know that you are strong enough to surrender to the unknown and survive the true state of who you are? Are you able to do this without the materialistic things you've been conditioned to want and need in order to make yourself happy and whole?

We've had it backwards the entire time. Everything material that we gain from this life is secondary. We should replace the big house, fancy car and picket fence with love, kindness, peace and unity. We should build ourselves inward and work our way outward instead of filling up with external things.

It's necessary to stop once in a while and pay attention to life because we're all part of the same consciousness. The world is slowly crumbling before us and as we continue through our everyday routines, we are walking further and further away from ourselves. It's imperative to look closely at ourselves, love ourselves, and find out who we are. Life will take on new meaning and we will fully appreciate its beauty.

Conclusion – Presence

"Do not be distracted by the noise of the world, the endless chatter, or even your own setbacks. Be patient, remember your purpose, and be guided by your heart." –Tena M. Dodds

The world will continue to hold our dreams, but it's our responsibility to execute the quality of our lives in the way we carry ourselves. We can continue to lead a life of worry, a life of making plans for how we wish to live. It shouldn't take a tragedy for us to reflect on how we can do better. We should always try to work our way from within to fulfill our lives by committing to always choosing this now moment over any past or future experience. Our fears limit what we can achieve, but we can let go of that fear at any time and re-create a new set of beliefs. It takes a lot of practice to live fully in the present moment. There are more people than not who are imprisoned within their thoughts and don't realize they have the power to free their minds to come into union with their body.

Today, everyone has been bitten by the reality of distraction, whether one is glued to social media, their television, or consumed by their job or other addictions. More people suffer from "text neck" because their full attention is on their phones instead of what is right there in front of their eyes. People in our society lack the tools to deal with feelings and have to search outside of themselves for happiness. People fall off cliffs taking selfies, or die from accidents because they were texting while driving or not paying attention while they were crossing the road. We have become robots, functioning to please an audience, to gain likes or views from others who are on the same road seeking validation.

Presence is an art form. It's a deliberate decision in the beginning of practice that evolves into a natural way of being over time. It's choosing this now moment over any other thought. It's being at one with life, allowing ourselves to feel whatever arises despite how intense. It's not avoiding how we're feeling, but having the courage to sit in those feelings without running away trying to fill the void externally. It's savoring each moment no matter how insignificant it may seem and making precious memories to save for forever. It's honoring our life and the journey it has taken to get us here.

Chapter 4

Love

"She lived and breathed love
Like it was imprinted deeply within her soul
And no matter how much life tried destroyed her
She knew love was the answer.
She knew love conquered all."

Karen A. Baquiran

Introduction – Love

"Change. I've certainly had my fair share of life-changing events, moments that made me question my existence. The biggest and most life-saving change came in accepting things as they are. In doing so, I stopped asking "why me?" and started accepting that it doesn't matter why, it's just my life's journey."—*Tena M. Dodds*

People can't help themselves if they're unable to recognize and admit that there is a problem. We're the sole creators of our reality and there are moments in life that reveal the truth of who we really are. Sometimes we feel lost and helpless and don't know where to look for the comfort we need to progress. The simple fact is that the Divine Love within us is the foundation of every living soul. But we fail to recognize that finding that Love is enough to lift us back into wholeness.

We all want to be loved and to be recognized as successful. We all want to be validated, and we continue the never-ending search for our soul's purpose. It's a never-ending battle in getting back on our feet to keep our composure in hard times. Sometimes we need to crumble to the ground and break all the barriers surrounding our true nature in order to get back up again. Over time, these barriers have locked us away from our true selves.

We want people to see us like we're held tightly together. We want people to see our confidence and we want to feel indestructible as if nothing in this world can harm us. When we can recognize that the foundation of Love within us is the vital part of who we are, this newfound clarity diminishes the false reality that material possessions make us successful and complete human beings. And only then can we finally see that there's so much more to our existence. We find meaning, we find hope.

Our power lies in knowing that behind every accomplishment, we are already whole starting from the beginning of life until now. We are all spiritual beings and in Awakening to this, we find that everything we were strictly conditioned to believe as part of this *life* is not a reality after all but, in fact, an illusion. We are each responsible for the happiness in our lives. Our minds are in the driver seat and in order to obliterate the false way of life, we need to change our thought processes. We need to think less with our minds and more with our hearts to bring love, peace, and kindness to our world, and we need to see that a full bank account will never buy us permanent happiness. Money is a necessity, but depending on it for fulfillment creates a deeper void that will never be satiated by material possessions.

If we train our mind to take one barrier down after another, we may now be left at a road block consisting of fear. But behind that fear is a choice. The choice is either to go further and seek Love, or put the barriers back up. Because this journey isn't always easy, it takes hard work to truly look inside your soul. We're so used to seeking that which doesn't fulfill us because that's the easy thing to do. It takes great strength and courage to face the fear of the unknown. But if we're strong enough, we'll recognize rock bottom as an opportunity for growth and not perceive it as the end of the world. Those who have recognized Love as their true essence will get hurt, but they choose to pick themselves up because their wholeness is enough to keep them steady and ready for what is to come.

We may meet people along the way who've been through hell and back but still manage to help others and keep a smile on their faces. With their authentic Love of self, they're already strong enough to fight for themselves through life's battles. We deserve to just be, to remain in a safe place that we can call home. We deserve the calm serenity of being still without moving or thinking or doing. We deserve to tell our fears to move to the side because we choose to be indestructible. All we need to do is believe in ourselves and imagine a life without the material things that society says will make us happy. Are we happy knowing that if we physically have nothing, we will be ok? If we say yes, then we're on the right track, but if we say no, we need to find our Love within. Finding your Love within allows you the safety of knowing with conviction your wholeness, knowing the Universe has your back, and that everything is going to be okay no matter what is thrown your way. Everyone is born with Divine Love at the core of who they are and that is a truth that we take for granted.

4.1 Love

"Outward appearances may be deceiving. You never know the struggle that hides behind someone's smile. Your neighbors, friends, and even family may seem like they have it all together but could actually be crumbling behind the scenes. So be kind always and never judge. Everyone is going through something." –Tena M. Dodds

No two home environments or life stories are the same. I've known many people who live their lives filled with any number of things including love, hate, discomfort, contentment, suffering, and everything in between. We never know what our neighbor is enduring or what they feel or what they've been through. It's so common to hear someone's story and be surprised by the details because they're so good at keeping up with appearances. And you wonder, how on earth do they hold it together?

Sometimes people lose themselves in their lives because of their suffering. And I wonder often how they find the strength to keep on going especially when their reality has been turned upside down. I've seen people judge others for the way they live and honestly I find it hard to understand how one lacks compassion. Some can be so quick to criticize and judge when they can't take the time to put themselves in another's shoes. We all have a story and sometimes our stories are tragic, but it's not meant for us to compare and judge another for the way they cope with life's difficulties.

I've been saddened to hear that one of my closest friends has experienced several life-altering events. It's a change that involves the deterioration of both her parent's health. This type of challenge requires patience beyond imagination and a lot of her time. She used to have all this freedom and now feels that the time she has is imprisoning her. She is now putting herself last because the needs of her elderly parents are now coming first. I've known her for many years and have listened to her stories but now knowing what she is going through makes me look at life in a different way.

I admire her strength and endurance because not many people would continue to do what she has to do. But I know that everyone has that strength in them and it's just a matter of pulling it together and taking it one day at a time. It's so much easier to judge someone for how they choose to live but I encourage people to take the time to listen and understand. The people we encounter everyday may be going through something that we may not be able to comprehend, and we shouldn't use our energy to be mean. Instead, we can try to be a little more supportive just by giving a few words of encouragement or offer if they need anything to ease the stress. Appearances can be deceiving and sometimes behind that friendly smile, is a person whose soul is ripped to shreds and whose world is turned upside down.

Most of us have been gossiped about and it's not exactly the best feeling in the world. We need to have more support for each other. If we don't know what to say, we can show them that we care in other ways. Everyone's home life is different from the next and as a human, what we feel and how we strive to survive this life, matters. A nice attitude and a friendly hello may be enough to revive someone and guide them out of any harmful mental state. It truly is up to us to change this way of life by fighting for one another instead of against. Our struggles are real and even if they're incomparable to each other, we should still find compassion and understanding to help our fellow neighbor. Be kind, be love, be exactly what you would want to receive when the going gets tough. It could be that simple.

4.2 Love

"Only you can control how you feel, no one can make you feel something if you don't let them. Choose to feel good, to feel joy, to be at peace in your heart and you'll be given more to feel good about." –Tena M. Dodds

No matter what happens to us, we should try to live our lives with love on our sleeve. We have to somehow believe that whatever happens is for the benefit of our own personal growth and we have a responsibility to pay these lessons forward by being the example of how we embody that love. We have an infinite supply of love within but that doesn't mean that we do not have boundaries with others. We can always send love to people who need it most, whether we feel they deserve it or not. It isn't about getting it back from anyone, but knowing that we have created a healthy and loving relationship alone and that we have the power to open up that well of love for ourselves at any given time. We do not need to seek love outside of us because we have built a solid foundation alone.

It takes a lot of work to start the process of self-care, compassion, and love. It takes dedication in believing we are worthy. Restoring our own self worth is vital because we should be able to validate ourselves. By building our empire within, no one can take anything away from us unless we permit them. When we become solid inside, with enough self confidence to stand alone, nothing can stop us from living our lives with our full potential. If we put our power in others to make us feel good, what are we to do when that person is gone? If we give others that power, then we also give them that power to take it away. We are in charge of the quality of our lives but by putting it in the hands of others, we become a prisoner to them by needing them.

Healing is a process and a sign that we are willing to cut the cords to what holds us back. I had a lot of codependency issues and I had to look at my core wounds that made me become this way. As women, we are taught at a young age that we need to serve others, that our needs are put last. The relationships I had made were reflections of what were modeled to me as a child. I was shown that we avoided talking about anything serious and if we had problems, we fixed it by serving, giving them gifts, and people-pleasing. That's how I felt I received my most love, by doing things for others and getting praised for it. I felt neglected and abandoned as a child, so wherever I could get love, I did my best to receive it by being an obedient, good girl.

We're taught to seek love outside of ourselves and it's not our responsibility to nurture ourselves. But our parents are supposed to be there to model that. I am not blaming my parents because it is a multi-generational and ancestral let down. No one really knows how to deal with their feelings and emotions. I had years of suppressed feelings because I wasn't taught how to cope nor did I ever feel safe to do so. As a child, if I cried, I associated that with not receiving love. I carried that unhealthy coping mechanism up into adulthood and sometimes I still feel awkward expressing myself because the old programs can be so deeply ingrained.

When I did a lot of introspection, I had to question everything. I had to question my actions and if they were done for the right reasons. Did I serve others for validation or because I wanted to? Did I have a hidden agenda behind my good deeds? Was I trying too hard to keep the relationships that I wanted by compromising my own needs over others? I won't lie. It was a bit of a mind-fuck because I didn't realize how damaged I was by my core wound of abandonment. We live so gripped by these fears that we aren't lovable and that the people we love most will leave us because we aren't worthy enough. So we overcompensate our actions to ensure we receive love as we learned to as children.

All those abandonment issues had to be looked at and I had to do a lot of healing on my inner child. What I had seen and felt as a child had been an accumulation of generations of old stories that developed my own sense of self. A pivotal moment of my healing journey came when I imagined being the last person on the planet. Now what? Who is going to love me now if no one is here? And the answer was me, the last person on the planet. We have to learn to love ourselves for exactly who we are, that we forgive and thank the past for what it's given us, and see that those traumas of neglect were gifts into developing our own sense of self. We cannot look at ourselves as a half in search for another half of a person to complete us. When we see it that way, we do not give ourselves that opportunity to heal the complete self or see that we are already whole. Two whole and healing people coming together makes magic happen. It is a process of collecting the pieces of ourselves that were once lost, putting them together to see the entire puzzle, and knowing that we will always be enough as we are, even with scattered pieces left on the floor.

Healing takes a lot of forgiveness, a lot of letting go, and a lot of patience. It takes a lot of time and devotion in re-creating a new and healthy relationship alone, without being enmeshed in a relationship. Our trauma and core wounding hold us back and the fear associated with these wounds stop us from taking a chance on something better. It's so vital in our recovery to be kind with ourselves and to listen to the way we talk to ourselves and how critical we can be. We have to really treat ourselves like we would a child, or a lover, because it can take an instant to damage a soul and an eternity to start fresh once again. I went all-in and started with a clean slate. I became hyper-aware of how I treated myself and what saved me in those times of loneliness was that I had to believe in myself and that the traumas I had faced were not my fault. I was only responsible for developing healthier ways of coping and to forgive at every turn. The shadows of our darkest skeletons are there to show us where we need love and nurturing, and when we finally give ourselves the attention and compassion, we can love fully because we have embodied the true meaning of Divine Love.

4.3 Love

"What is life without love?" –Tena M. Dodds

When we have love and use it in our everyday lives, whether it's for the self, for others, in our workplace, or our cooking, everything is so much better because of this simple yet powerful ingredient. We can feel when someone lives in a house versus a home. Love is a strong feeling and unlike other feelings, love is simply the most comforting and most powerful kind out there.

We've all been in a situation where we can feel somebody's tension. Negative feelings are so strong that anyone in the room can feel it. I think if we're able to exert negativity with such force, then we should be able to channel the same force to exert love. We should start to push our passions to the positive end of the spectrum so that we can shift our vibrations towards love.

Things sometimes happen unexpectedly but it's our reactions that determine the outcome. Instead of huffing and puffing and bitching and complaining, how about we shrug it off, genuinely smile about it, treat it like it's not the end of the world (because it's not) and focus on changing the negative into positive energy. We choose our battles and decide whether or not it's worth it to remain affected or let it go. Our attitudes affect the outcome of situations and even the quality of our daily lives.

I wish in life we could live in a drama-free environment. If only we had a little bit more patience, we would stop rushing, smile more, make more eye contact, talk to people, and connect with people. Imagine how amazing life would be? We should always look for the good in everything.

We can easily make the effort to walk our life's path spreading joy and love all along the way because we never know whose lives we may change just by being mindful of our thoughts and actions. After all, what makes life meaningful is the human connection. We should live with love and spread it to everyone we meet because the world really needs it now. Life will be so much better if we lived with a positive outlook. We are powerful beings and we need to recognize that the change starts with us.

4.4 Love

"The power of love starts with the self." –Tena M. Dodds

I encourage people to look at themselves in the mirror, and I mean really look at themselves. I can think of when I was a child looking at myself in the mirror. I'm a natural observer, so I've gotten to know every single part of my face. I look at myself now and I notice what has changed and what remains the same. I think loving ourselves is always a work in progress. We may love ourselves to a certain extent and then suddenly find something that changes our minds. But what is it that influences our perception of the self?

In general, we are so obsessed with what's imperfect about ourselves. We are always looking at flaws and imperfections when we should really be accepting everything that we are regardless of how it makes us feel or what others think. What is it that makes us who we are? We sometimes depend on other people to love us and validate us, but we should put the focus on loving and validating ourselves. We will never appreciate someone's compliments if we can't see it in ourselves.

I think it's so much easier to love everything else but ourselves because we're trained to focus elsewhere. It's almost a bad thing to focus too much on ourselves because then we're labeled as selfish or vain. I don't think it's selfish if it means nurturing our souls and accepting ourselves for who we are. I personally think if we can really love ourselves, we can love anything without any conditions. If the restriction of love starts with us, there is no way we can fully express our love outward. When we create a solid base of love with the self, then there are no longer any boundaries or insecurities. Knowing we are enough allows us to confidently love with our entire being.

We should pay attention to our flaws and recognize them as part of who we are because beauty is found inside and out, and love always starts from within. And when we finally master the art of self-love, we will illuminate the natural and flawless light that we are, a light that we once ignored.

We'll walk with enough confidence and it won't matter what anyone else thinks about us. When we receive criticism from others, their opinions are a reflection of the criticizer. Just remember that who you are is enough and the most important thing you will ever do is love yourself fully, madly, deeply. Embrace your perceived flaws as a part of you (we all have them), and let your authentic beauty shine through.

4.5 Love

"Life challenges can make us bitter and resentful. But being bitter and resentful is a choice. Let your pain make you soft, not hard. Compassionate, not cruel. Gentle, not harsh. Choose to be warm-hearted and loving. Take care of each other and be kind." –Tena M. Dodds

In my spiritual journey, I've spoken to many people who are kind enough to listen to what I have to say. I don't preach my beliefs but I do state my truth with examples to back it. They do see a difference in the person I've become and I feel the light that I have within me shines bright.

For a long time, I've felt different but it's only now that I'm awakened that I know where this feeling comes from. Bottom line is that I'm different spiritually and applying my practice to life has made the difference between who I was and who I am presently. I'm in constant evolution because of all the lessons that have been thrown at me.

I know I'm a good person so I wonder sometimes, why am I not friends with everybody? I've created boundaries because, in knowing my worth, I can't allow just anyone to be a part of the space of peace that I have made for myself. I've accepted that I can't please everyone and the only person that needs to be pleased is me. Any choice that I make has to be approved by me before anyone else and being comfortable with my choices will reflect in the relationships that I have.

Kindness is a choice. Some people are eager to treat perfect strangers better than their own family. That is a choice. Some people choose to not forgive and would rather make other people's lives a living hell. That is a choice, too, and they do this sometimes to either prove a point, or to prevent themselves from feeling inferior, or to simply make themselves feel better.

If we want to change our attitudes, we should treat others the way we want to be treated. Kindness should be practiced every day because just like changing our thought processes, we can start a change in the way we live our lives. A positive shift will occur in our minds, in our actions, in the way we interact with people, and in our lives in general. We should make the conscious effort to be kind to others without expecting anything in return. Our reward will come back to us through good karma. Life is so much richer when we live in abundance and generosity. Everyone deserves this, so it's up to us to make the difference.

4.6 Love

"How happy we are depends on how healthy our thoughts are." –Tena M. *Dodds*

Positive thinking can change our lives for the better. Clearing our minds of negativity and bringing in affirmative words and positive thoughts helps to establish a healthy mindset. A healthy mindset will then bring positive energy. And because positive energy will be part of our daily lives, failures or losses may be a bit easier to deal with. Potentially negative situations won't be as taxing and will be seen as a learning experience. With all the positive energy circulating, negativity will fail to cloud our minds and finding happiness will be effortless.

Because we sometimes fear rejection, failure, and other negative feelings or experiences, we tend to assume the worst in order to avoid being disappointed. It's easier to assume the worst because if things fail, then we avoid going through the sentiments of a letdown. Being positive and sending this energy out into the Universe will boomerang it back to us. When we are sure of something, saying it out loud and believing it will actually manipulate the way it gets sent back to us.

We may sometimes hear ourselves or someone we know say something along the lines of: "Knowing my luck, I won't win anything" or "Because it's me, nothing good will happen". Having these negative thoughts and believing them is the source of the bad luck. If we were to change these negative thoughts and envision the exact opposite of what was said, things would probably start to turn around.

We should have faith and trust in the Universe and try to feel good about ourselves and our environments. Love is such a beautiful remedy and we should allow it to fill our souls with its Divine strength and energy. We should allow it to be a reminder that there is good out there. If we are in a moment of weakness, we should surround ourselves with good people who love us and care for us and want the best for us. They can be our strength to help regain and revive the positivity in our lives until we are strong enough to sustain ourselves.

I always encourage people to selflessly pay it forward so when we are strong again, we can be the pillar of strength for someone else. We can live a better life if we free our minds from the things that do not best serve us. If we make the conscious decision to react differently, the negative things won't take over our minds and thus make space for happiness.

4.7 Love

"Up until now, you have survived 100% of everything you ever thought you wouldn't. Despite every time you said, "I'll never make it", you made it through. Every. Single. Time. If you have survived your hardest of challenges and darkest of moments and are still here to tell the tale then odds are you will survive whatever else life throws your way. Let your light shine through and hold onto your Love deep within. If nothing else, you have that and it is enough to pull you through." –Tena M. Dodds

We all want someone to love us or need us because then that means we have a purpose. Love is such a powerful motivating force that the desire to have it is a necessity to survival. I can't think of anything better to fight for because I know that when we are full of love and are surrounded by love, we feel indestructible.

It's so important for me to be able to nurture those in need. In my own desperate times, I knew what it felt like to feel neglected, and I wish that someone had genuinely been there. Having support now and being able to reflect on my life, I've learned to let go of my past and use my weapon of love to fight all negative things that no longer serve me.

I want my children to live in love and to be able to take this force with them in every journey they encounter. I want nothing more than for them to have the feeling of security and to know that they are safe. I know my son has a fierce love in his heart because of the way he carries himself and at 4 years old, he never hesitates to take my hand to kiss it and tell me he loves me. I'm his example and witnessing his true essence unfold without apology is a beautiful thing.

We may experience the true meaning of love when we go through periods of need. Through these times, we're able to witness love work its many miracles. Love is the force behind all things, in forgiveness and letting go, in sacrifice and surrendering, in patience and fighting darkness. Love conquers all if we just open our hearts to its powerful abilities. Knowing how to use it for the benefit of all is the ultimate way to express it and pay it forward.

We should look deep into our souls and allow love to come through because even when we're in desperate times and we feel completely helpless, that pull of freedom is love's way of telling us we've had it all along. We should look at ourselves and affirm every day that we are full of love. This allows us to become love and this Divine truth will shine through. We can let love be the leader of our lives and once we understand and believe in its powers, love will never fail us.

4.8 Love

"My life is not wasted if I have eased the suffering of even just one." —Tena M. Dodds

Patient care is the professional term for compassion. It's a very important aspect of my job as a radiation therapist because not a lot of people know how to be compassionate. Compassion is a specific art form that I have perfected in my many years outside the profession. In my job, compassion is a form of connection, of love, of positivity, and of understanding the human suffering within the confines of illness.

Compassion isn't necessarily about the words we speak but the way we emit our overall energy. Being able to control our energies and creating a calm space for our patients is one of the most important and vital parts of their care. They have to feel like they're safe, that we're trustworthy and welcoming of them into our space. Just making the effort to bring ourselves to some sort of understanding is so important in giving them the chance to feel that they're someone's priority. Most of all, they need to feel that they're not alone during their most vulnerable time.

I've seen people I work with lose their initial mission in being there for the patient. Sometimes it seems they lose sight of the patient's identity as a human being and just refer to them by the body part we're treating. We do some procedures that may take extra time and that sometimes causes concern for my fellow coworkers because they don't want to end their day late. It bothers me that they stop seeing the patient as a person because behind each patient is a story, an identity, and a soul who is going through a tough time. We are their healthcare providers and it should be our mission to remain true to the oath we took to give them the highest form of care.

People in the healthcare profession tend to lose sight of the bigger picture. We are there to save lives, to increase quality of life, and to offer emotional support when needed. Our connections to each other seem to be lost and what better way to connect than to look at our fellow human being and say, *"I'm here for you and I got your back. You can trust that I will give my full self to you so that you don't feel like you're just another sick person. You are under my supervision and you will receive the best quality of care that I can give. You are not alone. You are heard. You are seen. I am with you."*

I treat my patients with love and that makes such a difference. Love is the ingredient that changes everything so we should add it to everything we do. If we exude love with all of our being, our lives will be filled with love. If I can make my patient not feel like they're sick for the 20 minutes a day that they are under my care, I've done my job. This job has to be personal on some level, but not to the point that it becomes consuming. As health care practitioners, we have to feel good about what we've done and the patient has to feel good about what they've received.

We have to think about putting ourselves in other people's shoes and how we would want to be treated. How would we want to be seen at our most vulnerable? We don't have to go completely over the top but to just show some sort of understanding is already doing a lot. Patient care is hard if we just want our days to come and go. We may be the best at our jobs but if there's no personal care for the patients then we're only doing it for the paycheck. We should smile, make them feel at home, and create that positive space for them. We are responsible for keeping it together because their world may have fallen apart at their diagnosis. Compassion is often missing in healthcare and sadly, in life overall. It's up to us as healthcare professionals to make the changes necessary to bring compassion back to the forefront of patient care.

4.9 Love

"To love unconditionally is to make a decision, a commitment to love without judgment, without limits or boundaries. To love for no reason and to have the courage to give without expecting anything in return. To be there in the darkest of nights and the brightest of days and to be brave enough to open your heart fully and completely to a person who by nature is imperfect." –Tena M. Dodds

My younger sister, Pickle is going to give birth soon. We had her baby shower and like all baby showers (mine included) I can't stand them. I'm not a shower-celebration kind of girl. I guess it's because of the entire formality of it. However, when I stood back a moment to watch the party unfold, I was filled with so much love because of all the people who came to show their support for my little Pickle.

My sister was my little buddy growing up but I took our bond for granted. She was my kid sister who would do just about anything for me. I was a *role model* to her and somehow I feel bad because as an older sister, I wasn't always the nicest. I see the way she leads her life today and I'm proud but I never gave her credit for anything she has done for me. She has done so much and seeing her move into another chapter of her life is quite amazing to me because she has come such a long way. She will always be my little baby and I couldn't be prouder of the beautiful woman she's become. Seeing the number of people enter the door to honor her and her baby girl made me feel so happy and I appreciated the moment because she's one of the most important influences in my life.

I anticipate the arrival of my niece and as a family, we are slowly preparing and coming together to bring this new soul into our world. I'll be using my duty as aunt to be a better role model for my niece than I was for her mother. And I will make it a point to show my her a world of love and acceptance. We can't always rectify the past but when we know better, we do better. When the reflection is brought into our awareness, it is then up to us to make the change. We take for granted those that would move mountains for us and we sometimes fail to say a simple *"thank you"* or *"I'm sorry for not being that awesome."* It's never too late to move forward with our lessons. We should make a better version of ourselves each and every day.

The connections we make and the mistakes we learn from are what changes our ways of life. I intend on being a better example and I'll only do so with the greatest intention of love. My little Pickle will be a wonderful mother because she has so much love in her heart. In reflecting on our lives as sisters, it was Pickle who was the actual role model as she always remained loyal even when I was rotten to her. She was the greatest teacher of my youth and I couldn't be prouder. I love when I get these moments of clarity because now I can repay her for all she has done. Through my gratitude, I'm able to openly appreciate her and honor her and give her what she's always given me: the gift of unconditional love.

Conclusion Love

"I feel you whispering to my heart and my soul trembles, beautifully awakening to the unbridled passion of love." –Tena M. Dodds

She came from a prayer, a request I had made one lonely night. I felt like all the planets lined up when she came into my life. I had simply asked for a friend and somehow in the escalation of our newfound bond, we realized it had evolved into so much more. It's easy for people to assume that I left my marriage for someone else and that I fell in love with a woman but it wasn't that at all. I never asked to replace one relationship for another. I was desperate for a friendship, someone who understood the everyday woes of life, someone who I could talk to when I felt lonely in my marriage. I fell in love with someone who saw me for me. It was unconditional love and had nothing to do with the body, but the connection of two souls.

Have you ever had someone whisper to your soul? Someone who can make you tremble without having to touch you? It confused me but at the same time, it was the only thing that made sense in my life. I never asked to fall in love with another person. It wasn't my intention for that to happen. But it did. It kept me up at night because it blossomed so quickly and I had never in my life felt so free to be myself and she loved me through my transformation. We were in the same boat, both in loveless marriages and seeking something more in the lives we were limited to. We bonded over the wishes we had made, never to be fulfilled by our spouses. It didn't matter that we lived in a different country and we had obstacles in the way. What we learned in our long distance relationship was unconditional love has no bounds and that the feeling of separation was only an illusion.

The moment I felt I was loved deeply, I'm certain a chemical reaction occurred within me. I finally felt alive from the intoxication of how much love we had in a short amount of time. There was an undeniable feeling of acceptance when both our hearts combined and for the first time I felt like I could breathe because she loved me and nothing else mattered. She so passionately loved me that it started to heal me. I felt a lot of guilt, but I knew on a soul level that this was too good to let go. We could have decided that what we had was unthinkable because it was straight out of a love story that remained in the fiction aisle.

She was supportive in my decision to leave my marriage. I didn't leave for her, I left for me. We had no plans to start a life together; in fact we didn't even know if it would ever happen. The most important thing that happened in my decision was that I was serving my highest good, knowing very well that there was no guarantee of a life together. But it didn't matter to me, because I had her in my life and it didn't matter how. Her gift of unconditional love had given me the opportunity to finally express myself, stand up for myself, and love myself when I thought it was impossible. Her presence had made me face myself, to look at my wounds dead in the eye and she showed me how beautiful I was despite my fear to confront it. Her love was the bridge back to me. She embodied so much that I wanted to grow and I wanted to do and be better in life. I became fearless after meeting her and I am so grateful for the many beautiful gifts she has blessed me with.

This relationship was never about romance. It was so much more than that. I had discovered a passion I never knew I had and I let go of everything that stopped serving my life. I had turned the tables on myself and found the courage to unleash the goddess that she always saw within me. She knew my potential and believed in me when I never thought I could. She saw me for who I was and listened to me and gave me the safe space to be myself when I was too scared to show anyone who that was.

I always believed that if you are loved well, you will grow at an exponential rate that nothing can get in the way of. It was exactly that. When I met her, I felt like I was planted and she watched me bloom into who I am today. She had been there through the crucial parts of my healing journey, forgiven me many times when I had hurt her. She had mirrored me in so many ways that I couldn't run away from myself. She held me through the toughest moments of my life, breathing so much wisdom in my darkest hour. I had instantly changed the day I met her. She was sent to me by God and I knew I had done something right in my life if I had manifested my own earth angel. I count my blessings every day that I get to walk this earth knowing that someone like her loves me.

A Poem for Teen,

I felt my words were never enough to express the song my heart would sing for her.
She's everything I had always longed for;
Everything my soul had looked for in the many lives it had lived.
She was my perfect Sunday, a day where the sun was bright.
She was the brightness of the night sky, illuminating every star birthed across the Universe.
She was the needed breeze in still air.
She was the blossomed flower, the brightest colors to ever exist.
She was the much needed nap on a stormy day, the perfect cup of coffee on a cold winter's day. She was the reason I refused to sleep because I never wanted to miss a moment without her.
Her soul fed mine in ways that lovers never die.
Her love continuously created the lyrics, I desperately wanted to sing to her.
She was the reason I wanted to be better, why peace still existed, why love never ended.
She was the reason that caused my heart to beat, that caused the air to fill my lungs.
She was the calm in my storm, the colors that made a rainbow, the butterflies that built new life after the caterpillar ended.
She never knew the impact she had on me and maybe she will never know this truth.
To be the inspiration in my life is the greatest gift, to be so inspired to change the world, so powerful.
She's the most beautiful soul that graced the earth she walked on.
And what's amazing about her still is that she doesn't even know it.

Chapter 5

Gratitude

"She took a deep breath,
Inhaling the creation of her life.
And as she exhaled
She finally acknowledged her evolution.
Her growth brought her liberation.
And with gratitude on her sleeve,
She knew she was ready to conquer whatever else was to come."

Karen A. Baquiran

Introduction – Gratitude

"They say that seeing is believing but I believe the opposite to be true. When we believe in something wholeheartedly and have faith that the Universe will work things out, it is only then that we will see the true magic of life unveiled." –Tena M. Dodds

I remember the day I had my spiritual awakening. It was a few days before my 30th birthday and I bought one ticket to see Oprah in my hometown of Montréal. It was a gift I wanted to give myself and what came from that experience had changed the course of my life. It was the first time I was fully present that I was able to feel electricity running through my body. Oprah said something profound that night and it hit me like a ton of magical bricks. *"Stop looking at what you don't have and start looking at what you do have."* And that's all it took. Oprah gave me a verbal slap in the face that changed my perception, and instantly I felt a release of pressure for not having enough but felt this sense of appreciation for everything I did have.

I walked out of her show completely changed. I was feeling an excitement I never felt before and I was so excited to be alive. I felt motivated and ready to really grow up because of this newfound appreciation for life. The art of practicing gratitude has given me the ability to savor everything and everyone that has filled my life. I was always looking on the darker side of things, saying that I didn't have this or that and I wasn't worthy of any of it. Living in a state of scarcity only kept my perception in a state of lack. It wouldn't matter what I did have, because it would never be enough.

A change in perception can sometimes be the magical antidote to people's suffering. The way I viewed my life after that night changed so dramatically that I couldn't wait to see what else my life had in store. I made it a point to say *thank you* all the time and I felt instantly rich even though nothing had physically changed. My need for more had stopped and I put my focus on trusting that I would always be fine, that I had everything I needed, and it wasn't necessary anymore to panic when I had no reason to. I was a prisoner of my mind and I never had the capacity to even think my life would change that quickly. All it took was one powerful message that had been permanently implanted. That was a life altering miracle and I am forever grateful that I got my life back just by one change in belief.

5.1 Gratitude

"There is a vast amount of beauty in the transcendence of suffering. The most beautiful people in the world have transformed their pain, not into bitterness, resentment, or hate but rather into compassion, kindness, and love. Beautiful people do not happen by chance." –Tena M. Dodds

Suffering comes at a price and we sometimes lose a part of ourselves in the experience. The burden that we carry with us can destroy our lives, tarnish our self-worth, and through it all may affect our relationships. It takes a lot for us to move past the pain and re-establish ourselves. It is an intense journey to remove ourselves from the darkest days, and it takes great courage and faith to rise once we've hit rock bottom.

Suffering is an important lesson but through it all, it is possible to become a pillar of strength once our suffering is understood and overcome. When we rise above and move past our sorrows, we have a sense of appreciation for life and a knowing of how precious life truly is. The Universe will never give us anything we can't handle and in knowing this, we are our own greatest teachers. We are the examples that, regardless of whatever happens to us, we can still be patient, we can still show compassion for others, and we can still choose to smile, act kind, and find reasons to be happy.

We all have a story that makes us who we are and I've met many people in my life that have gone through tragedy after tragedy. What's incredible to me is that we would never know they've suffered because they don't wear their suffering on their faces and they don't allow their pain to define their lives. These people have found strength and courage to detach from their losses and what makes me admire them even more is that they have a thirst for life and live with an undeniable sense of humility. To witness this phenomenon is a miracle and it truly gives a deepened perspective because when I put myself in their shoes, it is so easy to assume that I wouldn't be able to survive the storms that they have weathered. At the same time, to have them as a model of survival gives me hope in knowing that even if one's life takes a turn for the worst, there's a calm at the end of every storm. I show gratitude to them as a way to honor the parts of them that they have lost and more importantly to honor the parts of them that have survived.

5.2 Gratitude

"When we lead with a grateful heart, the Universe conspires to give us more to be grateful for." —Tena M. Dodds

If we really want something, we have to believe that anything is possible. By believing in the law of attraction and in the work that we put in, we are opening ourselves up to receiving. I've been encouraged by my spiritual friends and guides to say positive affirmations that will help me to recondition my subconscious mind and develop a positive sense of self. These daily affirmations can help create a solid foundation of self-worth and gratefulness.

When we practice positive affirmations, (I am happy. My life is abundant. I am grateful for…), we can train ourselves into believing that what we're saying is an actual fact. And through this daily repetition, we will find that our perception will slowly evolve into a positive belief system. As we affirm these positive messages, we feel worthy and open to receive.

I started writing down goals and things I am grateful for in a journal. In writing and reading these statements, I am sending these thoughts into a Universal wishing well. I really encourage everyone to take the time to do this, as it only takes a few minutes out of our day. By keeping ourselves motivated through our goals and finding things to be grateful for, we are taking responsibility in creating our quality of life. The more that we are grateful, the more we are appreciative of what we have and what we receive.

We are responsible for this internal positive shift just by making the effort to find things to be grateful for and affirming it. All it takes is the power of gratitude and to let go of the outcome. Everything I've ever wanted had manifested through thought and intention alone. Receiving what we ask for comes when we least expect it, like a package we forgot we ordered. The power of manifestation has been a magical gift and I never thought my life would change so drastically if I never made the effort to believe in its life-changing abilities.

5.3 Gratitude

"Failure is necessary for growth." –Tena M. Dodds

I can't say that I have had many FML moments, but I can say that I've been able to survive my storms more gracefully now that I have experience. It is always in hindsight that we can take a look back and see everything without being so judgmental. It takes practice to become the observer in a situation instead of getting so consumed by our emotions. With this practice, it's easier to see the greater lesson instead of feeling sorry for ourselves. We can easily fall into victimhood, but when we can see that everything happens for us, instead of against us, we will be able to accept what is happening and be grateful for it.

We live through cycles where we experience ups and downs, triumphs and disappointments, but it is so important to be able to accept the bad just as equally as the good. We always call the people who have suffered the most the strongest, and that's true. Without these trials and tribulations, how else are we to test our own strength? No one wants to be in a sticky situation and no one wants to feel sad or upset. We only accept our happy emotions but how are we to appreciate the happy times, if we never experience the sad times?

Suffering comes less when we can acknowledge that everything is temporary. Everything is happening for the benefit of our life. We are the ones who are responsible for how we choose to perceive what is happening around us. We can take every lesson we've had and use it as a stepping stone for our future and pay those lessons forward to those with less experience. We have so many opportunities to teach others, to be the example of how to fall as gracefully as possible. It is so easy to feel sorry for ourselves and hate our lives so much because it hasn't been fair. On the contrary, we can take ourselves out of that bubble and see the greater picture as an outsider. From that standpoint we can release our emotional attachments and be able to be the observer. Not everything deserves a reaction. We are entitled to our feelings, but it can get toxic if we are manipulated by these feelings and act out according to our pain.

I used to avoid taking a risk at all costs because I was scared of failure. By not taking these chances, we are limiting our experiences and not giving ourselves a chance at possible opportunities. We aren't doing ourselves a favor by not taking a risk. Nothing in life is guaranteed and if we feel that we are making choices based on protecting our own feelings, we may not see what else this life has in store for us. It takes a lot of courage to make that jump regardless of outcome. I always feel that if we can stop fast forwarding to the result and be present in our lives, we can be grateful every step of the way because fear and failure are really just illusions and we can be proud that we took that chance no matter what.

5.4 Gratitude

"Sometimes it's so hard to love being alive when your days are filled with pain and exhaustion. But I always think to myself that there's someone out there dreaming of a life like mine. Someone with much less than I have that would love to live my life. So I'm grateful. I'm grateful for the little things. I'm grateful that I woke up today. I'm grateful that it's a beautiful day. I'm grateful that I have a place to call home when so many do not. I'm grateful that I have food to eat when so many are hungry. I'm grateful to have a few friends when so many are lonely. It's so important to love your life more than you hate your pain. Fall in love with being alive again and don't let your pain take away from your spirit. Life is still beautiful. You just have to see it, be grateful for it, and let the beauty of life live in your heart." –Tena M. Dodds

I am so thankful every day for my life. I am thankful for my good health and that my kids are happy and kindred spirits. I am grateful that I have a civil relationship with my ex-husband and that we are fortunate enough to provide for our children as single parents. I am thankful to have a heart full of love and that I have people in my life that I trust and respect. I am thankful every day because I don't know what tomorrow will bring and I can only imagine how I would feel if something were to change. Devastating things happen to people every single day. It's courageous to me that one would find the strength to continue smiling at the world despite the tragedies they have experienced. It is a huge lesson that when our own lives seem full of flaws, there is someone else in the world who wishes that they could have our *perfect* lives.

We should count our blessings every single day because we never know what we have until it's gone. We don't know the extent of someone else's life unless we put ourselves in their shoes. People suffer every day, whether it's because of their surroundings or because they have a mental and/or physical illness. We can only imagine how they cope, or how they put on a brave face because they don't want to burden anyone with their pain. We can only imagine how they have the strength to drag themselves as forward as their weakness will allow them to.

I admire these types of people. They are the real troopers who still act kindly and generously without expectation and who choose not to act from their place of hurt. They continue to give themselves to anyone because what more do they have to lose? It should be a lesson to those who take their life and health for granted. We never know what will happen down the line, which is why we should continue to thank our lucky stars for everything good that we've been blessed with.

Life can be a wonderful experience but sometimes it can be a huge slap in the face. We have the ability to adjust to whatever is thrown our way and we should be thankful every day for the countless blessings we have been given. And if we're healthy, we should be thankful that we are. We all have an original story to tell and what makes a great story is when we can live selflessly and honestly. A great story starts with love and ends with love and if one can remain grateful despite the downfalls, that is powerful to no end.

We should be kind to others because we never know if they're suffering. We never know that behind the genuine smile of the passer-by, may be a soul suffering with a painful body or mental anguish. We should be thankful for our lives today and always hope for a peaceful tomorrow.

*This message is dedicated to the millions of people who suffer every day. You are thought of daily and I can only hope for better painless days. You are not alone in your fight. Thank you for being my teacher. I am sending you an infinite amount of love and spoons.

5.5 Gratitude

"I think people often confuse forgiveness for releasing their offender from accountability. Forgiveness is not about the other person at all. Forgiveness is about you. It's about releasing the chains of anger, hatred, and resentment that weigh so heavily on your soul. It's about liberating your heart from sadness and grief to make room for peace and love to enter, for light to return to where darkness once flourished." –Tena M. Dodds

Today I'd like to take the time to express my deepest thank you for the many people whom I consider blessings in my life (family, friends, acquaintances, coworkers, strangers, and even enemies). But I want to focus my energy on the people who have come and gone and are no longer here.

I know that most folk are naturally eager to be angry and hate their enemy. That is what we're supposed to feel toward an enemy, right? I've been there and done that. I actually don't choose to hate anything as I'd much rather give my power to love. I will send my love out there to those that are no longer in my life because I feel that they still deserve as much love as the next person. No one is perfect, but I have an understanding that some may hurt others, not because they have an evil soul, but because it's clear that they are hurting themselves.

How many times have we talked badly about someone versus talking great about someone? We are quick to jump the bitch wagon if it means gossiping, trash talking, or saying anything and everything to make us feel better about ourselves. But if we think about it, how exhausting is it to wake up angry, drive mad, breathe hate, sweat resentment, wreak negativity, and wait for the next person to offend us so that we can attack? It's hard on the mind, the body, and the soul. When we live in negativity, negativity becomes us.

I am sending my love to the people that dislike or hate me because I truly only wish the best for them. It's not about being the better person but about liberating myself from what no longer serves me. When we reach a place of feeling comfortable in our own skin, it becomes second nature to know what we are worthy of, and what we deem acceptable to take into our life. I appreciate my old friendships regardless of what went down in the end. Life can get in the way, we can grow apart, or we let a disagreement come between us. I don't hold any animosity but love. With a heart full of love and gratitude, I am always free.

Conclusion Gratitude

"We are taught and conditioned by society to be helpless and to look for healing outside of ourselves when in fact everything we need to heal has been inside of us all along. If you're looking to be saved, the only person that can rescue you, is you. Be your own hero. The power is within you and it starts with loving yourself fully. Feel the power in your vulnerability and let it rise to the surface. That's where your healing will begin." –Tena M. Dodds

Sometimes we go through these phases where we feel like a dark cloud is following us. We may not necessarily feel depressed or mad or angry, but we feel that there is something a bit off. It kind of reminds me of a dull headache, tolerable but annoying.

What is the remedy to this annoying problem? Have we been in our heads a lot lately? Is it that maintaining our happiness has become a chore? It's ok to lose our sense of happiness once in a while because it is temporary. We should experience other things so that when we reach happiness, it's like arriving at a finish line. Happiness is the reward after a hard lesson learned and we should appreciate it when we reach it.

Getting off-track is completely normal. There will be instances that come and go and that will hurt us, annoy us or bother us, but these also carry the possibility of being temporary if we allow it. When we overcome these problems and learn from them, then we can be free from the burden of negativity and feel the freedom of love. We need to experience the vulnerable points of our journeys because without them, we will never be able to learn from them. Only we have the power to save ourselves. We may look to others for help or support, but we are the only ones who can free ourselves from these unsettling feelings.

I find myself to be in less crappy situations, but that's because I now choose my battles wisely. I am in a place where whatever happens, I've accepted as an opportunity to grow emotionally and spiritually. Every person that comes into my life has made an impact. Some impacts are stronger than others and I would rather hold onto something great than something sad. I'd rather talk about something real than something superficial. It's a matter of connecting more positively so it makes it easier to be happy. I choose my battles and when there is no battle to choose, I choose to live in the moment as neutral as possible.

Being off-track just means that I am human. We are sometimes taken off-track so that we may see other events more clearly. Sometimes we take for granted everything we love, so when things are going great for us, it would be a good time to show appreciation. When we show appreciation, we are taking the time to value what we feel empowers us and what makes us feel worthy.

Even when we're knee deep in a problem, know that it is happening for a reason and we can hold space for our happiness. When we find ourselves in a problem and our thoughts are consuming, everything seems impossible. But we shouldn't be afraid to feel our pain and allow the emotions to speak to us. By becoming in tune with ourselves, we become familiar with the parts of us that need more attention and nurturing. I've learned the hard way that feeling the full spectrum of our emotions is healthy and that even if we're squirming from an uncomfortable situation, it is only to better ourselves. It allows us to remain in touch with our authentic selves. We may feel down in the moment but know that these times come and go. Nothing is permanent. We can't run from ourselves, so we might as well face the hard times and courageously show up and rise. This is a natural part of life and the beauty of our evolution. I personally love when this happens because after I've learned the lesson at hand, I can stand back and reflect. Everything happens for a reason and I know that I came out a little stronger, a little more wiser, and extremely grateful.

Afterword

"Sometimes we live so deeply gripped by fear that we forget about love. Choose love. Choose to do more than exist. Choose life." –Tena M. Dodds

The journey to self-love can be such a strenuous process. Our real-life experiences are the elements that are strategically placed on our timelines as a way for the Universe to help us find our true authentic selves. Everything we endure is a test and after experiencing the calm that follows the storm, we find ourselves a little stronger, a little wiser, and a little more aware. We are all survivors. Though it may seem that some suffer a little more than others, we are constantly tested to see how we handle life in mind, body, and soul.

Our minds are what carry us forward and this is the biggest factor in how we ultimately choose to live. Our realities are based on our thought processes and the way we handle every situation, whether it be in how we view ourselves, our loved ones, our peers, friends, colleagues, strangers, society, or the world at large. We take for granted that our thoughts play a role in how we live and that the quality of our lives can change the moment we realize that we are always in control of the way we perceive everything.

Everyone has a lesson to learn and it certainly is a beautiful process when one is capable of opening themselves fully to the learning experience. Even our enemies serve a major purpose in our lives and though they may not serve us in the most positive way, they end up being some of our greatest teachers. Forgiveness and letting go are the harder lessons in life that many people struggle with. They would rather take their lifelong grudge to the grave than forgive their enemy. It definitely takes great courage and understanding to realize that forgiveness is for ourselves and not for the other person. The burden of our pains shouldn't be there to serve our ego. In its true release, one is able to remove the heavy weight of pain and resentment. When one is able and willing to forgive, the old place of burden is then naturally filled with love.

Loving ourselves is talked about but not many know how to go about it. It can be a long process because of the way society has been brainwashed into viewing how life is meant to be lived. We see it everywhere in the media and we lose sight of ourselves and who we are meant to be because of the pressure that is put upon us. We are trapped into thinking that we have to follow the simple equation to life that may include growing up, getting educated, starting our careers, meeting our partners, getting married, buying a house, having some kids, working until we're 65, paying our bills, retiring, and then dying. There is so much more to life than this equation but sadly, if someone is unable to reach every goal, they're considered a failure someway, somehow. These societal expectations get infiltrated within our own psyche and if we cannot live up to these so-called expectations, we can feel unsuccessful, inadequate, and worthless.

It's so rare in life to be taught how to be happy, and to know that happiness is an inside job and not what fills our bank accounts or the big house we live in. We are falsely taught that to be happy, one must have top-of-the-line everything, the biggest of everything, and the most of everything. However, are people really happy with what they have? By giving power to these material things to ensure one's happiness and wholeness, there is a loss of appreciation for what matters most. There will always be a never ending search for happiness if we continue to look outside of ourselves as well as an unknowingness of how to appreciate whatever comes into our lives. Putting value on these material things then causes us to oversee the value of gratitude, peace, joy, and connection with our fellow humans. By building a solid foundation within and knowing we don't need anything outside of ourselves to be happy, there will be a realization that none of this material stuff really matters.

We are taught to compete with everyone around us and we no longer see the importance of compassion and empathy. Most people only see separation amongst each other, when in reality, we are all striving for the same thing; to be happy and loved. We are trained to look outward instead of inward. We are trained to not deal with unfortunate circumstances because we can easily hire someone to assess the situation through therapy and social work, again looking outwardly to solve our problems. We are taught to look in the wrong places for validation and to judge others for not living life the way the rest of us have been told. We don't know how to deal with anything anymore because we are afraid of taking a step forward to fight for our happiness. So many people appear to be stuck because they are unable to trust the process. There is no trust in what life has to offer because our conditioning of life's equation is so deeply ingrained that no one thinks too highly of their greatest potential.

Self-love is vital to surviving because no one should look at life as a means to only exist. It should mean experiencing life to the fullest because it is our birth right. It should mean being our true and authentic self because we are perfect as we are. It allows us to seek our greatest potential and to recognize that we are all worthy of greatness. We are intricately connected with All That IS. We can change the way we think, live life with love and an open heart, complete random acts of kindness, open ourselves to vulnerability, feel our every emotion without judgment, and be present in this moment.

Tomorrow is uncertain but if we just give ourselves a chance to be, we can coexist within the cynicism we have all collectively contributed to. When we know better, we can certainly do better. We've been trained to think that our happy ending only comes when we've fulfilled the conventional route to success. However, the real route to success depends on the individual and not on the power society has in dictating what that happiness may mean to each of us. Happiness is an inside job and nothing that we can find outside of ourselves. By knowing this, we are now responsible for taking full accountability of our lives. Regardless of how that is achieved, whether conventional or not, what matters is that we honor ourselves by living kindly and authentically. This paves the way for others to feel safe to do the same. This is the beauty of true liberation; being so unapologetically comfortable in your own skin that no matter where you are in life, you are *home.*

Printed in the United States
By Bookmasters